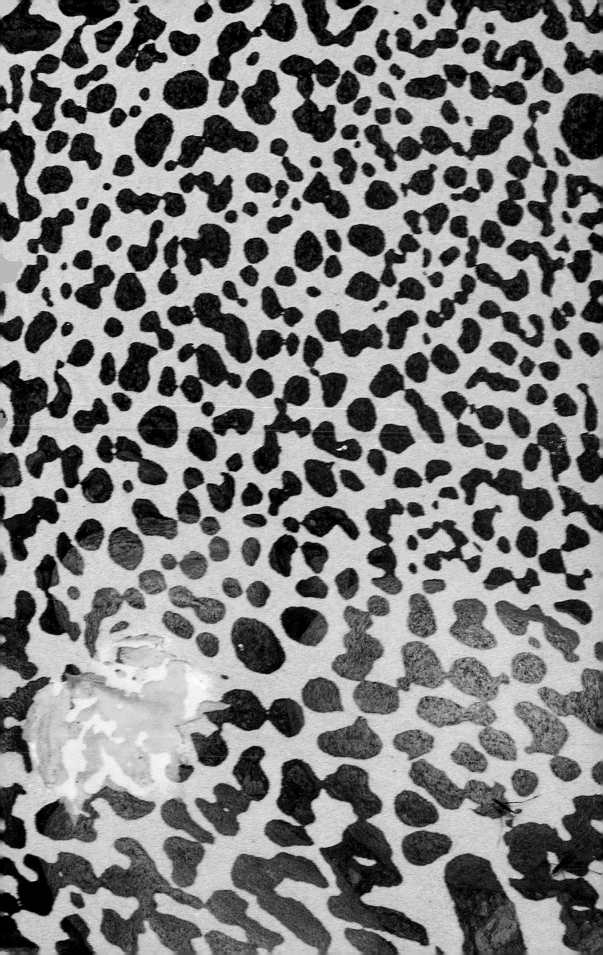

EXPLORING
CANADA'S
SPECTACULAR
NATIONAL PARKS

Photographed by Raymond Gehman

Prepared by the Book Division
Published by the National Geographic Society, Washington, D.C.

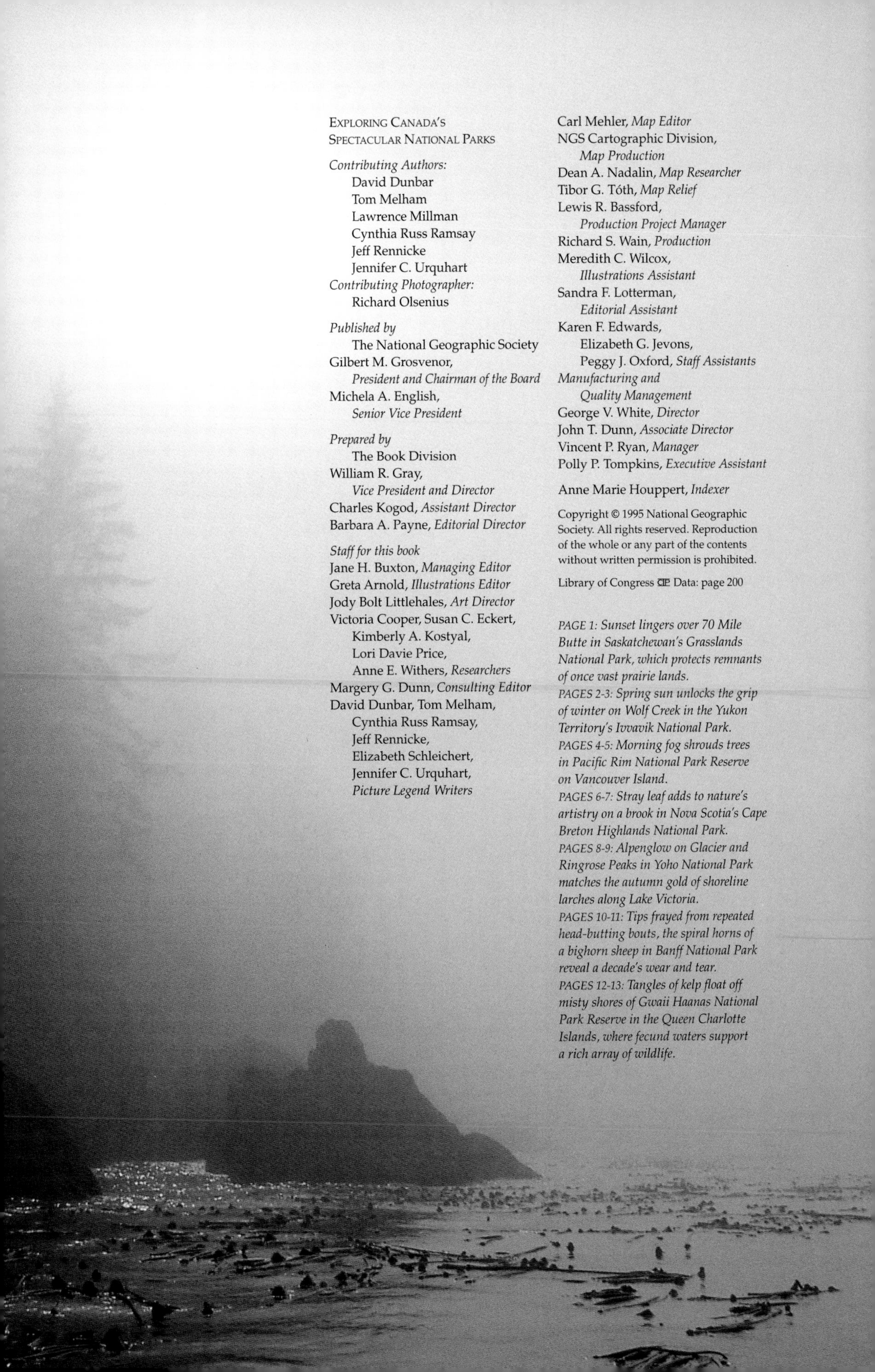

EXPLORING CANADA'S
SPECTACULAR NATIONAL PARKS

Contributing Authors:
  David Dunbar
  Tom Melham
  Lawrence Millman
  Cynthia Russ Ramsay
  Jeff Rennicke
  Jennifer C. Urquhart
Contributing Photographer:
  Richard Olsenius

Published by
  The National Geographic Society
Gilbert M. Grosvenor,
  President and Chairman of the Board
Michela A. English,
  Senior Vice President

Prepared by
  The Book Division
William R. Gray,
  Vice President and Director
Charles Kogod, Assistant Director
Barbara A. Payne, Editorial Director

Staff for this book
Jane H. Buxton, Managing Editor
Greta Arnold, Illustrations Editor
Jody Bolt Littlehales, Art Director
Victoria Cooper, Susan C. Eckert,
  Kimberly A. Kostyal,
  Lori Davie Price,
  Anne E. Withers, Researchers
Margery G. Dunn, Consulting Editor
David Dunbar, Tom Melham,
  Cynthia Russ Ramsay,
  Jeff Rennicke,
  Elizabeth Schleichert,
  Jennifer C. Urquhart,
  Picture Legend Writers

Carl Mehler, Map Editor
NGS Cartographic Division,
  Map Production
Dean A. Nadalin, Map Researcher
Tibor G. Tóth, Map Relief
Lewis R. Bassford,
  Production Project Manager
Richard S. Wain, Production
Meredith C. Wilcox,
  Illustrations Assistant
Sandra F. Lotterman,
  Editorial Assistant
Karen F. Edwards,
  Elizabeth G. Jevons,
  Peggy J. Oxford, Staff Assistants
Manufacturing and
  Quality Management
George V. White, Director
John T. Dunn, Associate Director
Vincent P. Ryan, Manager
Polly P. Tompkins, Executive Assistant

Anne Marie Houppert, Indexer

Library of Congress CIP Data: page 200

PAGE 1: Sunset lingers over 70 Mile
Butte in Saskatchewan's Grasslands
National Park, which protects remnants
of once vast prairie lands.
PAGES 2-3: Spring sun unlocks the grip
of winter on Wolf Creek in the Yukon
Territory's Ivvavik National Park.
PAGES 4-5: Morning fog shrouds trees
in Pacific Rim National Park Reserve
on Vancouver Island.
PAGES 6-7: Stray leaf adds to nature's
artistry on a brook in Nova Scotia's Cape
Breton Highlands National Park.
PAGES 8-9: Alpenglow on Glacier and
Ringrose Peaks in Yoho National Park
matches the autumn gold of shoreline
larches along Lake Victoria.
PAGES 10-11: Tips frayed from repeated
head-butting bouts, the spiral horns of
a bighorn sheep in Banff National Park
reveal a decade's wear and tear.
PAGES 12-13: Tangles of kelp float off
misty shores of Gwaii Haanas National
Park Reserve in the Queen Charlotte
Islands, where fecund waters support
a rich array of wildlife.

ARCTIC OCEAN

Queen Elizabeth

Islands

*Beaufort
Sea*

AULAVIK
NATIONAL PARK
(Proposed)

IVVAVIK
NATIONAL PARK

*Banks
Island*

VUNTUT
NATIONAL PARK

*Victoria
Island*

YUKON

TERRITORY

NORTHWEST TERRITORIES

Yukon

Mackenzie

KLUANE
NATIONAL
PARK RESERVE

*Great
Bear
Lake*

ARCTIC CIRCLE

★Whitehorse

Liard

NAHANNI
NATIONAL
PARK RESERVE

C A N A

Back

★Yellowknife

Thelon

*Great
Slave
Lake*

WOOD BUFFALO
NATIONAL PARK

BRITISH

Peace

*Lake
Athabasca*

*Queen
Charlotte
Islands*

COLUMBIA

R O C K Y

ALBERTA

SASKATCHEWAN

GWAII HAANAS
NATIONAL
PARK RESERVE
(Proposed)

Fraser

Athabasca

JASPER
NAT. PARK

Edmonton
★

PRINCE
ALBERT
NATIONAL
PARK

MANITOB

PACIFIC

Vancouver

Island

GLACIER
NATIONAL PARK

MOUNT
REVELSTOKE
NATIONAL PARK

ELK ISLAND
NATIONAL
PARK

Saskatchewan

*Lake
Winnipeg*

OCEAN

M
T
S.

YOHO
NAT. PARK

BANFF
NAT. PARK

Vancouver
●

PACIFIC RIM
NATIONAL
PARK RESERVE
(Proposed)

★Victoria

KOOTENAY
NATIONAL
PARK

●Calgary

0   400 mi

0   400 km

WATERTON
LAKES
NATIONAL
PARK

★Regina

RIDING
MOUNTAIN
NAT. PARK

★Winn

GRASSLANDS
NATIONAL
PARK
(Proposed)

*Parks that have not yet been included in Canada's National Parks Act or other legislation
appear as "proposed." Reserves designate parks subject to native land claims.*

Contents

ELLESMERE
ISLAND
NATIONAL
PARK RESERVE

*Baffin
Bay*

NORTH BAFFIN
NATIONAL PARK
(Proposed)

Baffin Island

AUYUITTUQ
NATIONAL
PARK RESERVE

Davis Strait

*Foxe
Basin*

D   A

Hudson Strait

*Labrador
Sea*

*Hudson
Bay*

Caniapiscau

N E W F O U N D L A N D

Churchill

TERRA NOVA
NATIONAL
PARK

GROS MORNE
NATIONAL PARK
(Proposed)

*Island of
Newfoundland*

★ St. John's

*James
Bay*

*La Grande
Rivière*

MINGAN ARCHIPELAGO
NATIONAL PARK RESERVE

*Gulf of
St. Lawrence*

Q U E B E C

FORILLON
NAT. PARK

CAPE BRETON
HIGHLANDS
NATIONAL PARK

O N T A R I O

R. de Rupert

St. Lawrence River

PRINCE EDWARD
ISLAND

PRINCE EDWARD ISLAND NAT. PARK

Albany

NEW
BRUNSWICK

★ Charlottetown

KOUCHIBOUGUAC NATIONAL PARK

Québec ★

FUNDY NATIONAL PARK

PUKASKWA
NATIONAL
PARK
(Proposed)

LA MAURICIE
NATIONAL
PARK

Fredericton ★

★ Halifax

NOVA SCOTIA

KEJIMKUJIK
NATIONAL
PARK

Lake Superior

Ottawa

Montréal ●

Ottawa ✪

A T L A N T I C

FATHOM FIVE
NAT. MARINE
PARK

GEORGIAN
BAY
ISLANDS
NAT. PARK

ST. LAWRENCE
ISLANDS
NATIONAL
PARK

O C E A N

Toronto ★

L. Ontario

Lake Michigan

L. Huron

BRUCE PENINSULA
NAT. PARK *(Proposed)*

L. Erie

POINT PELEE
NATIONAL PARK

FOREWORD

by Thomas E. Lee
Assistant Deputy Minister
Parks Canada
Department of Canadian Heritage

In the early 1970s, when Jean Chrétien was the Cabinet minister responsible for Canada's national parks, he took a trip up north. As the plane crossed eastern Baffin Island, the minister stared awestruck at the wilderness of spectacular fjords and ice caps spread out below. The man who is now Canada's Prime Minister said, "I will make these a national park…." A few years later, it happened. Prodded by the minister's personal passion for that beautiful corner of Baffin Island, Parks Canada made Auyuittuq our country's first national park north of the Arctic Circle.

Faced with the accelerating disappearance of unspoiled lands, the federal government in 1990 announced plans to complete the national park system by the year 2000—an undertaking that would require establishment of eighteen new parks, almost two a year. If that goal becomes a reality, Canada will end up protecting for all time nearly 125,000 square miles of wilderness.

This book, then, chronicles an exciting work in progress—Canada's national parks. Within its pages you can explore many aspects of Canada. The histories of our First Nations are well reflected in Grasslands, Gwaii Haanas, and Ivvavik. On the Atlantic coast, Gros Morne introduces the era of early settlement in North America and the remote and picturesque fishing villages of Newfoundland. In the Rocky Mountain parks you experience one of the world's great mountain ranges.

While our major international cities, Montreal, Toronto, and Vancouver, contain much of Canada's population, we are not yet, as a people, far removed from the forests, rivers, valleys, mountains, lakes, and oceans that have shaped the history of our young nation. Canada was founded in 1867 and established its first national park in 1885. Early in this century, it established a permanent national park service.

Canada's national parks have become much more than a collection of special places. They are a reflection of our people—our histories and cultures, our hopes and aspirations, our successes and failures. Our national parks capture and reflect our close relationship to the natural world and support the commitments that Canadians have made, both nationally and internationally, to support the global environment. Our task is not yet finished. Canada has an aggressive program to complete the task of setting aside representative areas of its natural heritage.

I wish to express my deep appreciation to National Geographic for producing this book on Canada's national parks. And I extend to all readers an invitation to visit, enjoy, and celebrate these special places of Canada.

Autumn makes a brilliant splash in Nova Scotia's Cape Breton Highlands National Park, which attracts 300,000 visitors annually. From precipitous coastal cliffs along the Gulf of St. Lawrence to an extensive highland plateau, the park encompasses many ecosystems.

PACIFIC
TRADITIONS

PACIFIC TRADITIONS

by Lawrence Millman

On a typically glowering, drizzly day in British Columbia's Queen Charlotte Islands, I asked a Haida Indian elder named Nathan Young to call up his memories of 50 years ago and more. Soon he was telling me a story about his uncle. The old man would stand on the deck of his fishing boat as it entered some cove or inlet in the southern part of these islands, which are known to the Haida as Haida Gwaii. Then he would gaze toward land and shake his head almost in disbelief, saying over and over again:

"Gwaii Haanas! Gwaii Haanas!"

Although Nathan Young's uncle did not participate in the naming process, Gwaii Haanas happens to be the name of the national park reserve that occupies the southern 15 percent of this far-flung archipelago. The words might mean "awesome place," "place of wonder," or "beautiful islands," depending on which Haida does the translating.

Yet whatever the exact meaning, one thing is clear: Those two words capture the essence of a realm that's like a cross between Arthur Conan Doyle's *Lost World* and the proverbial horn of plenty, with a dash of Alice's Wonderland thrown in for good measure. It's a realm where peregrine falcons whistle through the air at speeds upwards of a hundred miles an hour; where bald eagles build nests that can be six feet across and weigh nearly two tons; where black bears grow so fat during salmon season that their bellies drag along the ground; where those same bears, lifting up rocks in search of crustaceans, gently replace them, as if unwilling to disturb the ecosystem; where cyanide bugs smell of almonds; where sea lions, if you get close enough to them, give off a smell of ineffable rankness; where brown bull kelp can grow as much as a foot in a single day; and where a grizzly bear's monstrous grin adorns a Haida mortuary pole.

As befits a place of wonder, Gwaii Haanas has no roads or marked trails, and minimal development. No visitor facilities, either. And as befits a wilderness area, it is accessible only by floatplane, helicopter, or boat. For my own trip I chose the latter mode of conveyance in order to experience the park's 138 islands and 568 square miles as slowly and completely as possible. So in Queen Charlotte City

Low tide reveals a galaxy of bat stars and myriad other sea creatures in Burnaby Narrows. The intertidal zone in Gwaii Haanas National Park Reserve shelters some of the abundant marine life that has long tied peoples of North America's northwest coast to the sea.

PAGES 18-19: Hemlock branch offers a perch for a young bald eagle at Gwaii Haanas. A large population of these raptors, powerful totemic animals for the Haida, thrives here. PRECEDING PAGES: Sunset burnishes waters of Wickaninnish Bay at Long Beach in Pacific Rim National Park Reserve on Vancouver Island's west coast.

I chartered the *Kingii*, a 33-foot cabin cruiser, and set off on a voyage of discovery.

Quite early in this voyage, on the day the *Kingii* put in at Windy Bay on Lyell Island, I received a strong foretaste of Gwaii Haanas's wonder-making ability. It was a day even more stubbornly unwondrous than the day I visited Nathan Young. A cold rain was slashing away at sea and shore, mountains and forest. Likewise, a fog had crept in. Crept in not "on little cat feet," as a poet once wrote, but on the robust paws of a lion or a tiger.

Rain and fog—the meteorological two-step of the Pacific northwest. The former exalts flora to majestic proportions and swells up rivers so that salmon can swim upstream and spawn. As for the latter, it can draw a curtain of invisibility over whatever the former exalts. Fog and inclement weather have sometimes had a disastrous effect: Ships unable to see the shore have frequently ended up on it. In fact, there were so many shipwrecks on the west coast of Vancouver Island, south of the Queen Charlottes, that in 1890 a life-saving trail was hacked from the bush to aid survivors. The 45-mile West Coast Trail, now part of Pacific Rim National Park Reserve, roughly follows the route of the original trail. Nowadays the only wrecks tend to be hikers who negotiate the trail's countless mud sloughs, slippery logs, washouts, bridges, and 75 sets of rope ladders scaling cliffs and headlands.

But back to Windy Bay. However time-honored the weather, I was determined not to let it spoil my encounter with a place Haida artist Bill Reid once compared to the Peaceable Kingdom. So I donned my anorak, pocketed my compass, and went ashore. Soon I found myself walking through, if not the Peaceable Kingdom, at least a temperate variation on the theme of Amazonian lushness. Sitka spruces and western red cedars soared 200 feet or more into the sky, having cultivated rich mineral subsoils for thousands of years. Their roots now hunched up like gargantuan crab legs or sprawled out like gargantuan serpents. On the ground was a seemingly endless cushion of moss, squishing at my every footfall. Not content to cover only the ground, this moss crawled up the trunks of trees too. From the branches of these same trees dangled wispy green lichens called old-man's beard—a fitting complement, I thought, to an old-growth forest.

The fog lent an eerie quality to a world that was already stranger, much stranger, than the one I'd left behind. At any moment I expected to run into a *ga gixiid*. In Haida lore ga gixiids are demented, vaguely supernatural beings who inhabit the deepest, darkest parts of the forest. They can be easily identified by the sea urchin spines in their cheeks, by wide nostrils that flare dramatically skyward, and by their very long, very sharp fingernails. These beings specialize in the kidnapping of Haida who venture too far in the woods; and while not a Haida myself, I couldn't help wondering whether an overly zealous ga gixiid might forego the distinction as to my classification.

Instead of a ga gixiid, however, I kept running into fallen trees. They were everywhere, askew, aslant, and horizontal; they combined with ranks of dead snags to make my hike mainly an act of circumnavigation. At one point, more or less lost, I stopped to check my compass. And directly in front of me, moss-ridden, tapered at both ends, rotting but still distinct, lay an old Haida canoe at least 30 or 40 feet in length.

An astounding discovery! I stood in the rain, no longer hearing its persistent drip-drip-drip, and stared at this mossy relic. Once upon a time the Haida had paddled canoes similar to it hundreds of miles up and down the northwest coast of North America. Such canoes, piled high with sea otter pelts, bobbed year after year alongside New England trading sloops, until the sea otter was extinct in these waters. From mainland trade fairs they'd return filled with eulachons, a fish so rich in oil that, once dried, it becomes an instant lantern when one end is lit. Canoes would be used as ceremonial food platters at feasts and potlatches. And a canoe might even end up in a person's chest, whereupon a *nang sraagaa* (shaman) would be called in to exorcise it with a mystical massage.

But this particular canoe had never known the taste of seawater. It was at once dead, unborn, and derelict. I wondered how long it had rested here, untouched by human hands and unseen by human eyes, illuminated only by the green, subaqueous Pacific light. And why was it left unfinished? Had a flaw in the grain been discovered as it was being worked to completion? Or did the smallpox epidemic that ravaged these islands in the last century ravage its carver too? The only answer to my questions was the sonorous *c-r-r-r-u-u-k* of a raven in a nearby tree. Or maybe it wasn't a raven, but Raven himself, trickster-transformer of northwest coast legend. Raven created or stole—it was all the same to him— sunlight, trees, fish, water, dirt, and even sex. He also helped create the people who created this canoe. Or so the story goes.

Other Haida stories tell of cruel and unusual consequences suffered by those who do not respect nature and its denizens. A woman makes fun of a dogfish and slowly begins to turn into a dogfish herself. Two boys wantonly break the wings of bufflehead ducks and end up transformed into killer whales. A young man throws a live frog into a fire; a volcano erupts and destroys his village, killing everyone except an old woman and her daughter, both of whom had expressed sympathy for the frog.

Not surprisingly, I took care not to squash, crunch, or ridicule local fauna on my walk back through the woods. But I did mutter silent imprecations against the rain, now coming down in heavy buckets. At last, somewhat liquefied, I sloshed into Windy Bay. After visiting the remains of a 19th-century Haida lodge, I took refuge inside a modern lodge, albeit of traditional cedar-plank, post-and-beam construction, built right next to the older one. I entered this lodge in a highly unorthodox manner—through the doorlike pupil of a huge eye that was painted on the outside.

Built in the mid-1980s, Blinking Eye House was used as a base by the Haida during their protest against logging in the southern Queen Charlottes. Over the years various logging companies had sheared away much of the islands' luxuriant growth—old growth, new growth, ancient conifers, and upstart saplings. The Haida had occupied this increasingly shorn land for perhaps 10,000 years, back to the time of Raven himself. And they felt such a lengthy tenure gave them the right to call that land their own, their very own, and to evict tree-lopping intruders if they so desired.

At first the Haida protest seemed to fall on deaf ears. After all, the logging industry underpins British Columbia's economy. So the province has tended to take a dim view of those who bite the hand that ostensibly feeds them, even if that hand, in addition to feeding them, is messing up the environment. Never mind that logging can upset a rain forest's delicate nutrient and hydrological cycles and smother equally delicate aquatic habitats with bark and other debris; or that in its intensive, clear-cut form it can turn a landscape into a desolation of jagged stumps, craterlike holes, and crumpled earth. Never mind, indeed, when a single old-growth tree could be the equivalent in board feet of five houses.

As I huddled inside Blinking Eye House, I imagined the richly blanketed

*H*aunting reminder of the past, a moss-covered canoe (opposite) lies unfinished in the forest, perhaps because of a flaw in the log or because the carver had been stricken by smallpox. Skilled canoe makers, the Haida fashioned dugouts of red cedar up to 75 feet long to carry warriors and traders up and down the coast. Carved as many as 150 years ago, mortuary poles (above) at Sgan Gwaii village held remains of high-ranking dead. The southern Haida abandoned this site in the late 1800s, after disease decimated inhabitants. A sea grizzly on the pole at front holds a seal. Stylized creatures, real and supernatural, serve as crests of social identity. Even where remnants are less tangible than at Sgan Gwaii, such sites reveal the Haida's deep spiritual link with their homeland.

figures in the shadows—men and women, elders and youths, Eagle and Raven moieties, all dedicated to the salvation of their land from the chain saw. Some would be lamenting the loss of great cedars—the staff of Haida life—first on Talunkwan Island, just north of here, and now on Lyell Island itself. Others might be complaining about the rumble of logging trucks only a few miles from Windy Bay, an age-old silence violated. Still others might be talking about the arrest of 72 protesters who'd blocked a logging road at Sedgwick Bay in 1985. Or in hushed tones describing how one of the protesters—an elder named Ada Yovanovitch—opened her Bible and read this passage just before the police led her away: "I have fought the good fight, I have finished the course. I have kept the faith."

If this were a Haida myth, the loggers might be transformed into ancient cedars. So too would the provincial officials who enforced the wielding of chain saws in Haida land. But it isn't a myth. On the other hand, a significant transformation did take place on July 11, 1987, mostly as a result of national support for the Haida. On that date British Columbia Premier Bill Vander Zalm and Canadian Prime Minister Brian Mulroney signed a "Memorandum of Understanding" that led to the establishment of South Moresby National Park Reserve (any Canadian park subject to native land claims is called a reserve). Then another transformation occurred a few years later—the new park's name was changed to Gwaii Haanas, a name more in keeping with its wondrous aspect. More in keeping with its Haida aspect too.

Even though logging was halted, the Haida were still not satisfied. After all, they'd never given away or sold this land, much less earmarked it for later use as a national park. So they negotiated the Gwaii Haanas Agreement, which was signed on January 30, 1993. Not even Pacific Rim, which includes 21 enclaves of native reserves, is managed like this. The agreement requires a consensus on decision-making through a board that has equal representation in the administration of Gwaii Haanas. It creates an essential second line of defense—from the Tangil Peninsula south to Cape St. James—against the scorning of nature and its denizens.

Day after day, some dry, most wet, the *Kingii* nudged along the sheltered lee side of Gwaii Haanas, past places with names such as Huxley, Darwin, Faraday, Ramsay, and Murchison. Visiting the Queen Charlottes in the late 1870s, explorer-geologist George Dawson borrowed these names—all of which belonged to prominent l9th-century British scientists—and bestowed them on the local landscape in the manner of a man flinging confetti. But at least one of the names, Darwin, is not inappropriate for an archipelago often referred to as the Canadian Galápagos. Among its mosses, liverworts, flowers, amphipods, birds, and fish are some that are found nowhere else in the world. Or if they happen to be found elsewhere, they're located in the most surprising of places; for example, the liverwort *Dendrobazzania griffithiana* is known to occur only in the Queen Charlottes and the Kingdom of Bhutan.

If asked to name one of these islands myself, I might have named it after some eminent ornithologist. Or I might have skipped the eminence and named it after one of the multitude of birds I encountered day and night during the trip. Bald eagles were everywhere, peering down from their lofty treetop aeries. Endless squadrons of black oystercatchers would fly past and begin *pip-pipping* hysterically, as if I'd committed some horrible outrage. Once in a while a horned puffin would fly by and then turn its head as if in amazement at a fellow creature so weirdly constituted as to possess radar and a mast. There were ancient murrelets, rhinoceros auklets, Cassin's auklets, pigeon guillemots, fork-tailed storm-petrels, green-winged teals, red-breasted mergansers, red-necked grebes, pied-billed grebes, black-footed albatrosses, oldsquaws, and marbled murrelets.

At night I would camp ashore in moss-covered glades that were like topiaries

A fallen giant finds rest as a new totem pole comes to life. A beaver, crest of the Eagle clan, barely shows on a Sgan Gwaii mortuary pole (right). A new beaver emerges under skilled chisel strokes of Haida carver Wilfred Stevens (opposite). Recent years have seen a revival of old traditions and crafts among the Haida.

run riot. There I would be serenaded by the hammerlike beat of hairy woodpeckers foraging in dead trees. Or be awakened from my sleep by the *bonking* sounds of ancient murrelets as they banged into the old growth, falling to the ground, then trying to fly and *bonking* again. These birds head back to their burrows at night in order to avoid raptors such as eagles and peregrine falcons. Though ideally adapted for underwater propulsion, with short, stubby wings, they are not designed to fly in such a despairing entanglement of forest. So the birds attempt to make direct hits on their burrows, an act they invariably fail at, not being designed for sudden landings, either. But such seemingly bumbling behavior keeps them from being an eagle's dinner.

One day the *Kingii* ploughed into an enormous raft of sooty shearwaters in Hecate Strait, the shallow body of water that separates the Queen Charlottes from the mainland. The shearwaters had dined not wisely but too well on krill and were now so heavy that they couldn't take off. As I watched these avian obesities flap their wings helplessly, I noticed the water pulse and boil, then become silvery. A school of herring was also attracted by the krill. Then misty plumes announced the arrival of a pod of humpback whales. Soon the humpbacks were frolicking, leaping, diving, and swiveling, apparently unaware that it's bad manners to play with one's food. Their mouths, when they opened them, were literally red with krill. One whale seemed to wink its eye in my direction, as if to say: Quite a show we're putting on, isn't it?

Near Murchison Island we dropped anchor in a forest of lush golden kelp. Below the boat lay a sea that bloomed like the tropics, fueled by the interaction of the cool Pacific with warmer, nutrient-rich freshwater runoff from the mainland. Opalescent nudibranchs floated in slow motion like pieces of intricate jewelry liberated from their earthbound coffers. Anemones wriggled their finespun plumes to the rhythms of the tide. Stippled red crabs skittered back and forth along tongues of kelp as if on missions of the utmost importance.

Starfish came in such a variety of colors—dark blues and purples, reds and browns, yellows and oranges—that they seemed to be competing with one another in some sort of intertidal beauty contest. I observed one even more flagrantly purple than the rest and reached down to pick it up. Try as I might, I couldn't pry it loose from its rocky home.

Kingii is Haida for "Always looking into the sea." Which describes exactly what we did for the next few hours, wading around and plucking various edibles from the water. Terry and Charlotte Husband, the *Kingii*'s skippers, cautioned me about collecting rock scallops and other bivalves, because of the danger of red tide. But we did fill a bucket with crabs, "gum boot" chitons, red and green sea urchins, turban snails, limpets, and sea cucumbers.

That evening we sat down to a meal so enriching that, upon finishing it, I felt like seeking out a black bear—the Queen Charlotte Islands have among the world's largest—and wrestling it into submission. I had my chance to meet a black bear the following day. I'd been searching for a marbled murrelet's nest near De la Beche Inlet. A mile or so inland, I ducked under a spruce log, whereupon I found myself face-to-face with a bear seated happily in a berry patch. Both of us did double takes, just like a pair of comics in the movies. Then I backed quickly under the log; the bear itself crashed off into the bush.

A while later I figured that enough time had passed and the bear would be safely gone, so I stooped under the log again (it lay directly across the path). I came out on the other side just as the bear was returning to its former spot. We performed a second set of double takes, then I retreated a second time. But rather than risk a third rendezvous, I now made my way back to the boat. For I had a strong suspicion that an otherwise docile animal might not appreciate this sort of silliness. And it might show its lack of appreciation by wrestling *me* into submission.

At Hotspring Island I found myself in hot water again. Literally hot water. The island's eponymous springs boast temperatures that range from 89°F to 170°F. Settling into one of them, I entered a state of parboiled bliss. Several minutes later I was joined by the Haida Gwaii watchman, the native caretaker of that island. We sat there silently until I happened to mention the half-finished canoe I'd discovered on Lyell Island.

The watchman told me about finding a similar canoe himself a few years ago, on Burnaby Island. Then he added: "You can't walk more than a couple of feet in Gwaii Haanas without stumbling on some trace of our past."

As the *Kingii* continued her journey, I began to realize that the watchman's statement was not an exaggeration. At virtually every stream mouth or cove, I saw old house pits, fire pits, lodge beams, bark-stripped trees, or fallen totem poles that had become nurse logs for future trees. Numerous shell middens proved that the Haida had used the same intertidal banquet table we'd used ourselves, only they took advantage of its year-round bounty for centuries, *dllgus* (digging sticks) and *kit'uus* (seafood spears) always at the ready.

Some of these sites would have been no more than seasonal camps. Others, such as T'anuu, were once substantial villages. In 1878, when Dawson visited it, T'anuu was the most flourishing settlement in the Queen Charlottes, with 16 longhouses, each occupied by an extended family, and 30 totem poles rising above its wide, expansive beach.

Then the smallpox epidemic took its toll (the Haida holocaust, it's been called, because it reduced the population by some 90 percent). After seven years the village was abandoned. And as I walked around what was left of it, accompanied by Wally Pollard, T'anuu's watchman, I could see only depressions in the ground and rotting timber. T'anuu was too ruinous even to be called a ruin, too close to oblivion for my mind to reconstruct it. Indeed, moss—the epidermis that covers all things both great and small in these parts—was already blurring the distinction between a human environment and a bryophytic one.

The same was true of Gwaii Haanas's non-Haida sites, which were no less ruinous, although considerably more recent, than the Haida ones. All that was left of Lockeport, a turn-of-the-century mining community and later a salmon cannery town, was a battered trailer and a scattering of whiskey bottles. Rose Harbour's whaling station could be recognized only from its rusting boiler hulks and pier stumps. Two collapsed 1960s hippie shacks remained on the eastern shore of Burnaby Narrows. Ikeda Cove, a thriving copper-mining settlement between 1906 and 1920, was a ghost town; its grand hotel, a refurbished Yukon stern-wheeler, had become an indeterminate corpse of wood and metal. At Jedway the most intact object I could locate was an old commode chair, standing forlornly in a spruce thicket. And Jedway Bay, the site of a Japanese abalone cannery from 1910 to 1913, was a hodgepodge of terminally rusted metal behind which stood a solitary grave marker with the word "SAYONARA" written on it—a perfect epitaph for all these deserted places.

And yet I did not find such places or even the Haida sites especially sad. Poignant, perhaps; but not sad. Rather, they seemed part of an enduring cycle by which Man born of Woman, or Woman born of Woman, has but a brief time— maybe a few years, maybe an eye-blink of centuries—on these bounteous shores. Then nature will take over again, oxidizing metal, breaking down wood, and covering scars with a mantle of the richest green.

At last we threaded the needle of Houston Stewart Channel and crossed several miles of open ocean to Anthony Island. Here was situated Sgan Gwaii village, Red Cod Island Town, Gwaii Haanas's pièce de résistance and a place remarkable enough to be ranked with Egypt's Pyramids and the palace of Versailles as a UNESCO world heritage site. And what a location for such a site: Anthony Island dangles on the edge of the continent, miles from the nearest town or city, seemingly poised to be swallowed up by the vast Pacific. Instead of swallowing it up, however, the Pacific can lash it with winds in excess of 100 miles an hour.

As we anchored a few hundred yards offshore, I studied this 395-acre tract of rock and Sitka spruce. Except for its wind-whipped and thus slightly tilted tree line, it looked no different from most other west coast landscapes. But then Terry and I hopped into a Zodiac, motored around a barrier island, and lo, 16 totem poles stood silently before us like a row of exclamation points. A few were propped up by clamps and supports; several had ferns sprouting like cockades from their tops; a couple rested on pads of gravel; and all were bleached gray by the relentless elements. Even so, they had the appearance of sentinels from a distant era miraculously transported to the present.

And upon walking ashore I had the peculiar sensation of being watched by a veritable bestiary of faces. There were eagles, black bears, grizzly bears, killer whales, beavers, and gigantic frogs. Some had bulging eyes and protruding tongues, others grimaced in decay, yet others were broken or crippled but still somehow capable of powerful scrutiny…especially of a Gore-tex-clad anomaly like myself. Not being chiseled from heroic cedar, I felt like an intruder at an intimate, totally private gathering.

Once upon a time this village of watchers had been the stronghold of the Kunghit, a band of southern Haida equally renowned for their artistic and warlike qualities. They would descend in a lightning raid on a village like Skidegate and then vanish into the fog, having taken men as slaves and women as wives. They'd also take scalps as trophies; and if there wasn't time to take a scalp, they'd simply take the entire head. Beginning in the mid-1780s the Kunghit engaged in the maritime fur trade, benefiting greatly from their southerly location. From European and Yankee traders they acquired axes and adzes, possibly even block and tackle, tools that helped them give a monumental dimension to their totem poles and longhouses. Yet their culture, even as it prospered, was falling victim to the very influences that fed its prosperity. A social order that stretched back to the time of Raven began to collapse. Then smallpox struck. Ironically, when the last of the Kunghit left Sgan Gwaii in the 1870s and 1880s, they relocated to Skidegate, home of their former enemies.

The only surviving descendants at Sgan Gwaii of this once mighty people are the poles themselves. And peering at their acrobatic columns of faces, I wondered what they betrayed of the Kunghit mind-set. Did they show the legendary Kunghit pride? Or perhaps an aptitude for commerce? Or maybe an aptitude for fierceness? Reflexively, my hand went to my scalp.

Wanagan, this site's watchman, kept my imagination firmly in check. A bright, highly articulate man, he was a virtual encyclopedia of Haida lore. For more than 20 years he'd been coming to Sgan Gwaii not only to guard the site against vandalism, but also to educate visitors like me. And as both protector and teacher he was the original inspiration behind the watchman program. But even Wanagan found it hard to resist Sgan Gwaii's rather unusual atmosphere. He would arrive here by himself, for example, and then discover that he wasn't by himself at all—the spirits of the past always seemed to hover nearby, going about their daily tasks, gathering shellfish, stripping bark, laughing, and occasionally even crying.

As we wandered from pole to pole, Wanagan explained that "totem pole" is actually a misnomer, at least as far as these particular poles were concerned. Most were mortuary poles. They were erected to honor and hold a deceased family member or chief, whose remains—after a suitable period of mummification—would be packed into a carved cedar box and then put in a rectangular chamber at the very top of the pole. He pointed to a heap of bones 17 or so feet above my head. And as I looked up at these bones, I couldn't help but think how much nicer it'd be to enjoy one's eternal slumber perpetually aloft like this, close to family and longhouse, than to be stowed under the hard ground perhaps miles from home.

The animals incised into the poles were not monsters or demons, Wanagan said. Nor were they deities whom the Haida worshiped, contrary to the opinion of early missionaries. Instead, they were exclusively held crests of social identity and rank, somewhat like a European coat of arms or a Scottish tartan. Crests of the Raven moiety included the raven, killer whale, grizzly bear, and mountain goat, while Eagle crests included the eagle, frog, and beaver. Each crest told a story about how the dead person gained the privilege of its use by his family's contact long ago with the animal itself.

"Can you tell me one of the stories?" I asked. Wanagan shook his head. The stories had vanished with the Kunghit themselves and were now lost, lost forever.

We approached the stumps of several poles that had been shipped off to museums and galleries some years ago. To Wanagan, this was not unlike wrenching a person from his home for no reason and then clamping him in jail. "Those poles were born in Sgan Gwaii," he declared. "They should be allowed to die here." And the poles that remained were in fact slowly but surely dying here, buffeted by the wind, scoured by salt spray, and eaten by wood-boring insects. Many Haida think this is as it should be, since these skyscrapers of wood were not created to last forever. In the old days, when one of them toppled over, it was ceremoniously removed during a potlatch, and the pole was then cut up into many pieces that were distributed to high-status members of the same clan. But some Haida think the poles might gain a few precious years of life if a ceiling were placed on visitors to Sgan Gwaii. Just such a quota system restricts the number of hikers permitted to use Pacific Rim's West Coast Trail. And few seem to object to it,

*C*urious harbor seal surveys Echo Harbour on the west side of Darwin Sound. *Marine mammals flourish in Gwaii Haanas on plentiful fish and other sea creatures.*

least of all the plants and animals who've inhabited Pacific Rim for thousands of years, long before the Vibram sole invaded their territory.

It was now growing dark. I began walking away from the site, past the ruins of longhouses with names like Thunder Rolls Upon It House and People Think of This House Even When They Sleep Because the Master Feeds Everyone Who Calls. Before I climbed into the Zodiac, I turned for one final look at the poles. They seemed almost human in the twilight, like stoic, elderly gentlemen who'd seen much, borne much, so I murmured a polite good-bye to them. There was no reply, not even the hint of a reply—only the faint whisper of wind in the Sitka spruces and the call of a raven far, far away.

*G*reen algae carpet rocks in Salmon Creek (opposite) on Moresby Island.
Black-tailed deer browse on Hotspring Island (below). Facing no predators, the prolific
introduced species threatens native vegetation.

PRECEDING PAGES: Fog rolling in off the Pacific cloaks rocky outcroppings at
Puffin Cove, where storms sometimes bring winds in excess of 100 miles an hour.
FOLLOWING PAGES: Cedars and spruces bend low over branches of rockweed
to meet their own reflections in Rose Inlet off Houston Stewart Channel.

*V*ivid splash of color, a bat star edges across green algae called sea lettuce at Burnaby Narrows. These

nutrient-rich waters sustain a rare wealth of marine life.

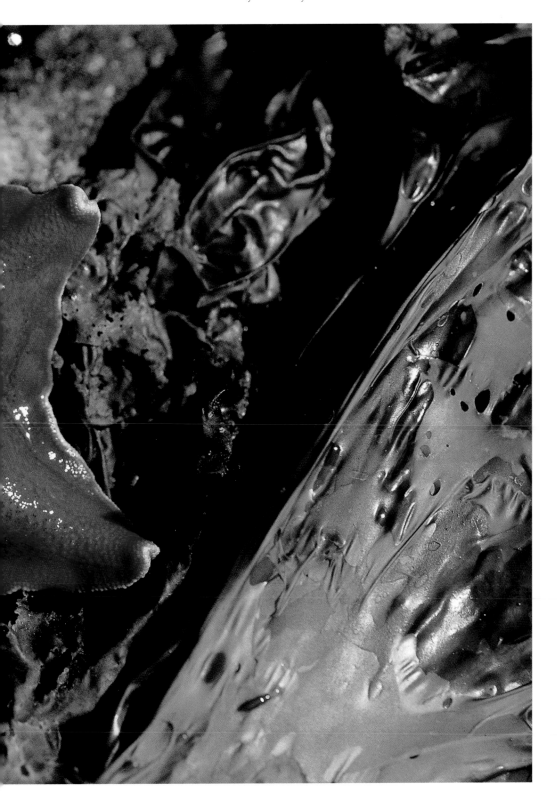

*S*teller sea lion bull and cow commune at a haul-out known as Skungii Nung, or "Crying Rocks," named for the moaning sound of the wind as it blows through a hole in the rocks near Anthony Island. Gwaii Haanas has one of the largest Steller sea lion breeding rookeries on the west coast of North America. A pair of pigeon guillemots (below) chatters on another outcropping after feeding on fish in the early morning.

FOLLOWING PAGES: The San Christoval Mountains on the islands of wonder and beauty known as Gwaii Haanas seem to float in a sea of clouds.

MOUNTAIN
ADVENTURE

MOUNTAIN ADVENTURE

by David Dunbar

In a letter to outfitter Fred Brewster in 1924, a guest at Jasper Park Lodge wrote: "At this greatest national park…not to follow the trails ahorse would be like visiting Paris and avoiding the Louvre and Versailles…the lure of your faithful trail-horses is the very life of Jasper." And so it was that I found myself on a sunny September morning astride a faithful steed named Jeff, riding along through a forest of Engelmann spruce and subalpine fir on the north slope of Mount Edith Cavell.

Guiding nine greenhorns from Japan, California, New York, and Great Britain into the southwestern pocket of Jasper National Park was Wald Olson, a pale-eyed, poker-faced outfitter whose family has organized pack trips in the park for some 40 years. Our destination on the three-day outing was the Tonquin Valley, one of the most scenic areas in the Canadian Rockies.

We descended into the Astoria River Valley, crossed the rushing stream on a log bridge, then switchbacked up crumbly Oldhorn Mountain, where rock slides have cut vast swaths of forest. As we broke out of the forest below Mount Maccarib, the Tonquin Valley came into view. We pulled up the horses, and silence descended over our polyglot group as we drank in the view. More a broad mountain pass than a valley, the three-mile-long Tonquin is carpeted with tussocky meadows interspersed with islands of spruce and fir. At the crest of the valley, the aptly named Amethyst Lake laps scree aprons at the base of a 3,000-foot vertical barrier known as the Ramparts. This glowering fortification forms one of the best-defined sections of the Continental Divide. Aboriginal peoples believed that fearsome beasts inhabited these ten peaks of Precambrian quartzite, some of which bear formidable names such as Dungeon, Drawbridge, and Bastion. The moat of Amethyst and the ice-crowned battlement soaring above it seemed to epitomize the wild, remote grandeur of the Canadian Rockies.

The most spectacular scenery in the Canadian part of the range fills four contiguous national parks. The man-made and natural attractions of Jasper, Banff, Yoho, and Kootenay are icons recognized around the world: the turrets of the baronial Banff Springs Hotel rising above the pines alongside the Bow River; the

Dusted with September snow, the Ramparts rear above spruce-fringed Moat Lake in Jasper's Tonquin Valley. Some eight million people a year explore four contiguous preserves—Banff and Jasper in Alberta and Yoho and Kootenay in British Columbia.

PAGES 46-7: Mount Huber (left), Mount Victoria, and Mount Lefroy, 11,000-foot peaks along the Continental Divide in Yoho National Park, loom beyond a silhouetted pine. PRECEDING PAGES: Its magnificent rack hoary with snow, a bull elk strides through an October storm near Vermilion Lakes in Banff National Park.

emerald waters of Lake Louise; the dazzling glaciers of the Columbia Icefield; the ridgeline of Jasper's Mount Edith Cavell.

The parks cover some 7,800 square miles along the Continental Divide in Alberta and British Columbia, one of the largest areas of mountain parkland in the world. Yet even these vast preserves protect only 11 percent of the Canadian Rocky Mountains, which extend from the foothills of Alberta west to the Rocky Mountain Trench in the interior of British Columbia, and from the U.S.-Canada border to the Liard River, 850 miles northwest.

These parks are intimately linked geographically, and no single Canadian preserve contains such varied topography. At the edge of Banff and Jasper's eastern boundaries the foothills rear up into the wall-like overthrust front ranges of the Rockies, which march in a series of limestone ridges and shale valleys into the heart of the parks. Along the western edges of the parks rise the ice-mantled peaks of the eastern main ranges, steep-sided, castellated mountains along the Continental Divide, composed mainly of tough quartzite and limestone.

In long, narrow Kootenay National Park on the British Columbia side, two wide, parallel valleys lie between three western main ranges, deeply folded mountains made of soft, easily eroded shale. Yoho National Park, north of Kootenay, is the smallest but most spectacular alpine park in the foursome, with 22 peaks of the western main ranges higher than 10,000 feet.

Eight million people a year explore these magnificent and varied landscapes. The Trans-Canada Highway and three scenic parkways—the Bow Valley, the Icefields, and the Banff-Windermere—take "windshield tourists" over passes and down broad, U-shaped valleys, past waterfalls, glaciers, and turquoise lakes. Drivers at dawn and dusk are often rewarded with glimpses of moose, elk, bighorn sheep, mountain goats, and other wildlife.

Day hikers fan out from townsites and campgrounds. Backpackers follow some 2,000 miles of trails to hidden canyons, flowered meadows, and remote passes. Anglers land trout in alpine lakes; climbers scale mountains; birders flock to montane valley wetlands in hope of sighting some of the 188 species seen frequently here. Rafters, canoeists, and kayakers run mountain rivers.

Winter brings downhill skiing at Banff, Lake Louise, and Jasper. Cross-country skiers glide to remote corners of the parks. Ice climbers inch up North America's best and most accessible array of frozen waterfalls.

Out in the Tonquin Valley, our three days were filled with quieter pursuits. One morning I rowed on Amethyst Lake while a fellow saddle-sore equestrian dropped a line for trout (the lakes yield up to eight-pounders). Another afternoon I hiked south to tiny, perfect Outpost Lake in the neighboring Eremite Valley. On an early evening stroll looking for moose, I saw a storm paint a fresh rainbow of colors on the drab flanks of Oldhorn Mountain. One night I watched from my cabin porch as lightning on the British Columbia side of the Great Divide backlit the Ramparts with brilliant flashes.

The scene was powerful, if fleeting. It reminded me of the 1924 letter to horseman Fred Brewster comparing trail riding through the park to touring the Louvre. I had followed the trails ahorse through nature's galleries to one of Jasper's masterpieces, the Tonquin Valley.

Jasper shares another of its scenic wonders, the Columbia Icefield, with Banff National Park. Sprawling 125 square miles along the Continental Divide, this vast deep freeze is one of the larger expanses of snow and ice south of the Arctic Circle.

From the valley-bottom Icefields Parkway, the Columbia Icefield appears as a thick layer of snow spread like cake frosting atop a massive block of limestone between Mounts Andromeda and Kitchener. To mountaineers who ascend outlet glaciers to the frozen heights, the ice field is something quite different, a gently undulating white plateau circled by some of the higher summits in the Canadian Rockies, the cloistered realm of a winter that has lasted two million years.

On previous visits, my appreciation of the ice field had been limited to windshield views. For a new perspective, I drove south on the parkway from Jasper into Banff National Park, then hiked up Parker Ridge, zigzagging through open meadows and isolated stands of subalpine fir into the alpine zone. At one turn in the trail, an outcrop of black limestone studded with fossilized white corals presented stark evidence that 370 million years ago this vertical landscape resembled Australia's Great Barrier Reef.

As I reached Parker's broad, treeless bench, swirling mists began closing in. I hurried over a small rise to a knobby limestone outcrop that hung off the side of the ridge like a gargoyle from the facade of a cathedral. A thousand feet below, the Saskatchewan Glacier reached through a rocky portal between 11,318-foot Mount Andromeda and 10,095-foot Castleguard Mountain. The Saskatchewan is one of the ice field's six major outlet glaciers. Braided meltwater streams trickling from the glacier's toe gathered on the floor of a forested valley to form the silver strand of the North Saskatchewan River, starting out on its 1,600-mile journey via the Nelson River to Hudson Bay. When cloud and mist curtained my million-dollar view, I reluctantly returned to the parkway.

For a closer look at the Columbia Icefield's glaciers, I drove north back into Jasper National Park and wound half a mile between gravel ridges, boulders, and meltwater ponds to the terminus of the Athabasca Glacier. This four-mile-long fissured finger of ice sweeps down between the north side of Andromeda and 11,449-foot Mount Athabasca and the south side of round-topped Snow Dome, an aptly named 11,548-foot giant with a gleaming skullcap.

Ungainly, fat-tired buses called Snocoaches take sightseers down a lateral moraine, then lumber out onto the ice. I opted instead for a glacier walk led by Peter Lemieux, a witty, bearded former park naturalist.

In the busy "Toe of Glacier" parking lot, Peter effortlessly memorized the names of his 13 clients while giving a brief safety lecture. Suitably outfitted in hiking boots, hats, gloves, and sunglasses on a warm, brilliantly sunny September day, we stepped onto the wintry Athabasca Glacier. Crunching dutifully on the granular snow in single file, we were surrounded on the lower glacier by slipping and sliding tourists in T-shirts, shorts, and sneakers. I felt overly cautious until Peter pointed to a spot where a German tourist had slipped into a crevasse a month earlier and died of hypothermia—just 66 feet from the toe of the glacier.

We walked over the uneven surface, quickly leaving other visitors behind. From a distance, the Athabasca looks dazzlingly white. Close-up, the glacier is a dirty gray from atmospheric dust, pollen, and ash from distant forest fires and volcanic eruptions. Peter guided us past rushing surface streams to turquoise millwells—vertical shafts drilled deep into the ice by summer meltwater streams. He identified cirque glaciers, which scoop out rocky bowls on the side of Mount Andromeda, and unstable ice towers called seracs at the base of Snow Dome.

Sparing no expense with pedagogical aids, Peter sacrificed a candy bar to illustrate glacial features. First, icefalls. Peter bent the candy bar near one end, cracking the bar's hard chocolate coating. The same thing happens when a glacier

*P*addles look puny against the roiling waters of Jasper's Maligne River (below).
Park officials ban human activity on the rapid-choked waterway from May through June
to protect riverside breeding grounds of harlequin ducks. Downstream, the Maligne
surges through the most spectacular slit canyon in Canada's mountain parks (opposite).
Slicing into massive limestone, the river has carved a serpentine gorge up to 165 feet
deep and, in places, only 7 feet wide.

flows over a cliff in the bedrock; a steep icefall is formed, its face creased with cracks known as transverse crevasses. Chomp. There went the icefall.

Next, marginal crevasses. Like rivers, most valley glaciers flow faster in the middle than along their margins, where friction with valley walls and the thinning of ice reduce speed, causing a shearing action. Peter demonstrated the effect of differences in the glacier's rate of flow by holding one side of the bar firmly in place and pulling on the other side. Diagonal cracks appeared in the chocolate coating, much as they do on the surface of Athabasca Glacier.

Chomp. End of lecture.

Chocolate crevasses led Peter into a story about a novice park naturalist who went backpacking with a more experienced colleague over the Saskatchewan Glacier to visit Castleguard Cave at the base of Castleguard Mountain. With 12 miles of explored passages, this cave system is the longest in Canada. Its passages extend northwest beneath the Columbia Icefield, nearly a thousand feet below the base of the ice cap, which is itself as much as 1,250 feet deep.

Near the toe of the Saskatchewan Glacier, as his partner forged ahead, the young naturalist fell into a deep surficial stream. Rushing water carried him into a shallow crevasse and under the ice. The near-freezing torrent swept him down a pitch-black tunnel in the ice with just a few inches of clearance beneath the roof. Within a few seconds that must have seemed an eternity, the tunnel began to glow faint green, then icy blue. Just as the naturalist became captivated by the colors, the stream flushed him out into the bright sunlight at the toe of the glacier. Shaken and shivering, but glad to be alive, he looked around and saw that he had beaten his partner down the mountain.

The name Yoho is a Cree expression of wonder, amazement, and awe. Relatively tiny Yoho National Park (506 square miles, or one-eighth the size of Jasper) frequently generates this spirited response with its spectacular alpine scenery. The most enthusiastic "yoho" is usually reserved for beautiful Lake O'Hara, south of the Trans-Canada Highway in the shadow of the Continental Divide.

Restricted access, camping and bus quotas, and a limited number of roofed accommodations protect the fragile beauty of the lake and its surroundings. These measures also ensure a high-quality experience for the 8,000 visitors who come each year to marvel at 11,000-foot peaks, valleys, meadowlands, waterfalls, and 25 lakes in every shade of blue. Those lucky few are either campers, day-trippers, or guests at Lake O'Hara Lodge or two huts operated by the Alpine Club of Canada. To reach O'Hara, you hike seven miles on a gravel road or ride a bus that makes the trip four times a day in summer. (Winter visitors ski or snowshoe in.) I took the bus to the lodge, an eight-bedroom, two-story cedar-and-fir chalet built during the winter of 1925-26. Eleven lakeshore cabins and four larger hilltop cabins complete the scene.

Lake O'Hara Lodge inspires such passionate loyalty that guests have returned annually for 10, 20, 30 years. Some people come again and again to enjoy the lodge's relaxed rusticity and gourmet food, and are content to admire the sublime scenery from lakeside. But most hike the network of trails designed primarily by George Link, a professor of botany at the University of Chicago, who came here every summer from 1928 to 1977—50 consecutive years. While building the trails, Link conversed with the ghostly presence of his wife, Adeline, who died in 1943—not surprising in a setting that inspires almost mystical feelings of transcendence.

The first thing I did upon arrival was to launch one of the lodge's canoes. Intent on preserving the dead-still silence, I carefully stroked O'Hara's crème de menthe waters, keeping my paddle well away from the gunwales. As I glided toward the center of the lake, I was astounded by the intimate scale of the setting. Barely two miles in circumference, the lake is cradled at the upper end of a narrow valley. A half dozen hanging valleys and glacier-carved amphitheaters radiate from the lake. Higher yet, scree fans out in broad cones at the feet of soaring mountain walls of the Great Divide, glittering with glaciers.

Docking the canoe, I set off on the 3.2-mile Opabin Plateau circuit, hiking through a mossy forest past Mary Lake and scaling the cliffs that define the northern lip of the plateau, which is actually a hanging valley. A side trip to the Opabin Prospect gave me an unimpeded perch from which to see, far below my hiking boots, the waters of O'Hara and Mary. At 6,614 feet along the Continental Divide, O'Hara gets a great deal of weather. During my circuit the sky drizzled,

Trail riders depart Jasper's Tonquin Valley via Maccarib Pass. Environmentalists complain that horses trample streambeds, degrade trails, introduce exotic plants into the backcountry, and spread the parasite that causes "beaver fever." Outfitters defend a popular and traditional park activity. Wrangler Kable Kongsrud (opposite) takes a trailside break with his dog, Blue.

cleared, and drizzled again as I wandered south through spongy tundra meadows. An American dipper bobbed and wove like a punch-drunk prizefighter on the bank of an outlet stream to Hungabee Lake, one of the plateau's numerous pools and ponds. As I reached Opabin Lake at the foot of Opabin Glacier on the upper plateau, the clouds parted, the sun came out, and I saw the summit of Yukness Mountain for the first time. With clouds scudding by its snowy crown, the peak seemed to be steaming like dry ice.

To protect critical grizzly habitat, Parks Canada closed the McArthur Creek Valley south of Lake O'Hara to hikers during my stay. In fact, the move may become permanent. "That would be gutsy in such a popular hiking area," said biologist Cam McTavish, who has been studying Yoho and Kootenay's grizzlies for three years, "but it may be essential." During an evening talk at the campground just down valley from the lodge, McTavish noted that North America's grizzly population has dropped by half in its Canadian range, primarily due to habitat loss and hunting. It came as a surprise to learn that the seemingly vast contiguous mountain parkland is too small to protect the entire ranges of such large carnivores as wolves and grizzlies. A grizzly's home range covers an astounding amount of real estate—more than 950 square miles over the lifetime of a large male. In order to maintain a healthy grizzly population, which McTavish defines as at least a thousand animals over several hundred years, the Rocky Mountain parks would need to be at least three times their present size. "Obviously, that's not going to happen," said McTavish. "If grizzlies are to survive here, the national parks will have to work with adjacent provincial parks, resource companies, and local governments." Case in point: During a 1988-91 study in Kootenay and Yoho, 5 of 11 collared bears were shot by hunters outside national park boundaries.

I reluctantly abandoned O'Hara's amazing scenery to join a guided walk to Yoho wonders of a much smaller magnitude on the north side of the Trans-Canada Highway. After hiking all morning, I stood on a ledge about 10 feet wide and 90 feet long, halfway up a ridge between Mounts Wapta and Field. Two hundred feet below, the Highline Trail was a faint scar across subalpine meadows. In the distance, Emerald Lake resembled a jewel tucked into the velvety green folds of montane forest. Beyond gleamed the glacier-capped President Range.

Mel Reasoner, educational director of the Yoho-Burgess Shale Research Foundation, had escorted eight hikers here on a restricted tour, not to admire the scenery but to see firsthand the world's most celebrated fossil bed, the Burgess Shale. (The tours, limited to 15 people, are given once a day.) Stepping around mountain goat droppings, we entered the quarry and rummaged through mounds of shale discarded during the summer's dig by students under the leadership of paleontologist Desmond Collins of the Royal Ontario Museum in Toronto. Nearly every cast-off slab we examined was imprinted with a fossil.

As early as 1886, railway workers had reported finding "stone bugs" in the rocks of Mount Stephen, just on the other side of the Kicking Horse River from where we stood. In 1909 Charles D. Walcott, who was Secretary of the Smithsonian Institution, split open a slab from the Burgess Shale and found a crablike creature he named *Marrella*. During the next decade, Walcott shipped some 65,000 specimens back to Washington, D.C.

The slab I looked at also bore the remains of a *Marrella*, a three-quarter-inch-long, eyeless creature that swarmed in shallow Cambrian seas some 515 million years ago. To the uninitiated, the fossil hardly looked remarkable, a finely detailed black film on gray rock. Yet *Marrella* was part of the early Cambrian "explosion of life," a burst of zoological evolution within the space of a mere 10 million years when virtually all the designs of animals living today came into being.

Most fossils are of hard-bodied creatures. Remarkably, the Burgess Shale also preserves the rarely found fossils of soft-bodied marine creatures, including a number of animals that don't fall comfortably into the 20 to 30 modern phyla, or groupings, based on body design. This tiny quarry contains the ghostly imprints of more different body plans than can be found in all the modern oceans.

For 40 years Walcott's fossils gathered dust in drawers at the Smithsonian's Museum of Natural History. Then in 1966 paleontologists from the University of Cambridge in England began to reexamine the specimens and, using high-contrast photography and other modern analytical tools, discovered bizarre and beautiful details hidden from Walcott. *Hallucigenia,* a worm-like oddball, had two rows of spines, perhaps one for locomotion and the other for feeding. The circular mouth of fearsome *Anomalocaris,* an 18-inch-long cross between a stingray and a lobster, was filled with hard plates and teeth.

The findings fired up a debate over classification that still simmers. Walcott described the Burgess fossils as early versions of animals that are still around today—sea cucumbers, worms, and arthropods. Harvard professor Stephen Jay Gould considered some unique creatures deserving of their own phyla. According to Desmond Collins, new fossil finds in the Burgess Shale and in China may prove that some of Walcott's disputed identifications were, in fact, correct.

A few days later and ten miles east of the Burgess Shale, the parking lots of Chateau Lake Louise in Banff National Park were overflowing with vehicles from all across North America. Down by the lakeshore, a man wearing a Tyrolean hat and lederhosen blew a ten-foot-long alpenhorn to amuse a group of tourists. The notes of "Amazing Grace" (misplayed) echoed off the walls of Fairview Mountain as I trudged along the lakeshore path in the rain, passing a hundred people in 45 minutes.

It occurred to me that a century ago Lake Louise must have been similar to Lake O'Hara, before highway access and tour buses. Back then, the forerunner of today's mammoth chateau was a chalet that catered to naturalists and alpinists, much as Lake O'Hara Lodge does now.

But in these four mountain parks, solitude often lies just over the next ridgeline. One valley south of Lake Louise (and just on the other side of the Great Divide from Lake O'Hara) was the aptly named Paradise Valley. There, I had a backcountry trail to myself for most of an overcast September day.

In late afternoon low clouds over the mountains that enclose Paradise pelted me with hail, then shrouded the world in a gauzy veil of big white flakes. Walking through a larch grove, I nearly stepped on a spruce grouse in the middle of the trail. The chicken-size bird took its own sweet time wandering off to peck at frozen berries. The grouse's indifference to my presence recalled stories of aboriginal braves so disdainful of the "fool hen" that they refused to hunt such easy prey.

By the time I reached the campground at Horseshoe Meadows the clouds began to rise like a curtain. In the heavily overcast skies, all I could see beyond the campground had been a moraine. Now, all of Mount Hungabee loomed into view, complete with a corona of clouds. Mists clung to a conical peak called the Mitre. About five miles north, hundreds of guests settled down for the night at the chateau. Here at the campground, five tents quietly sprouted.

The four Rocky Mountain preserves owe their existence to tourism, a spin-off of the national dream to build a transcontinental railroad. Once the Canadian Pacific Railway (CPR) had completed the coast-to-coast ribbon of steel in 1885, the company began to market the natural wonders of "Canada's Switzerland."

Locomotives of the day weren't powerful enough to haul dining cars up the steep mountain grades. Instead, passengers took their meals in special cars set on sidings. It was an inefficient way to feed the burgeoning number of riders, so the CPR built the great castles of the Rockies, Banff Springs Hotel and Chateau Lake Louise, as well as smaller edge-of-the-wilderness retreats such as Lake O'Hara Lodge. Soon hiking trails threaded the wilderness around Lake Louise, Lake O'Hara, and Banff townsite, and in Yoho Valley. Outfitters provided guests with hunting and mountaineering expeditions, trail rides, and motor launches for cruises on mountain lakes and rivers.

By 1920 all four parks had been established, not to protect the integrity of significant ecosystems but to preserve the unspoiled landscapes upon which tourism depended. In the post-World War II years, outdoor recreation in the "Mountain Playground of the World" and its attendant service centers were as much a part of the Canadian Rockies experience as the mountains themselves.

Today's heavy visitation complicates efforts to balance tourism with preservation of an ecosystem of international significance. (In 1984 UNESCO designated the four parks and three adjacent provincial parks as a world heritage site.) The twin mandates of Canada's 1930 National Parks Act, which stated that "parks shall be maintained and made use of so as to remain unimpaired for the enjoyment of future generations," was amended in 1988. The act now stipulates in addition that "maintenance of ecological integrity through the protection of natural resources shall be the first priority when considering park zoning and visitor use in a management plan." Furthermore, a 1994 park policy document states that "protecting ecological integrity and ensuring commemorative integrity take precedence in acquiring, managing, and administering heritage places and programs....Human activities within a national park that threaten the integrity of park ecosystems will not be permitted."

"The way I read the updated National Parks Act and the new park policy," said Ben Gadd, a respected former park naturalist, "it's quite clear that the parks are not intended as playgrounds or engines for economic development. They are supposed to preserve huge natural landscapes awesome in every way, and to be taken on their own terms."

Gadd and other environmentalists are alarmed when Jasper officials even agree to evaluate a proposal to permit expansion of a golf course in the montane forest, the park's most critical—and most altered—natural community. Or when park officials approve plans to build a housing complex on the site of a Columbian ground squirrel colony covering several acres in Jasper townsite. Even trail rides, "the very life of Jasper," are criticized for damaging hiking routes and for spreading exotic plant species and *Giardia lamblia*, the parasite in horse droppings that causes "beaver fever."

Park officials counter that the golf course proposal was submitted in conceptual form in 1992, when park management plans and the national park policy did not preclude expansion of existing golf courses. In addition, public consultation and an environmental assessment will precede any decision. The park service notes that there are other ground squirrel colonies in the Athabasca Valley and, anyway, the species is abundant and not endemic. Although park officials have no intention of banning trail riding, they continue to review ways to minimize the impact of horses on the environment and other park users.

Developmental pressures are even more powerful in Banff, which is just a 90-minute drive from Calgary (population 750,000) and its international airport. Issues facing Canada's most popular park include whether to limit commercial and residential growth at Lake Louise, whether to allow the Banff Springs Hotel to expand its golf course, and whether to proceed with turning another 11 miles of the Trans-Canada in the Bow Valley into a divided highway.

In the first two phases of twinning the highway, six million dollars were spent to build fences to reduce the roadkill of moose, deer, bighorn sheep, and elk. In 1983, the first year of the fences, elk fatalities were reduced from 55 to 1. Sounds good, but you can't draw hasty conclusions when it comes to fiddling with nature. It turns out that elk crop the grass on the outside of the barrier, leaving a luxuriant growth on the road side of the fence to support booming populations of mice and voles. The rodents attract coyotes, which wriggle under the fence, only to be killed by vehicles at a rate that equals or exceeds the rate of mortality of an "exploited animal population" that is being hunted and trapped.

Certainly, congestion on the Trans-Canada Highway, especially in summer, increases the risk of accidents. But building a divided highway in the richest, most productive habitat in the park is hardly giving priority to ecological integrity.

After the backcountry, a visit to Banff townsite is a near urban experience. On

Inquisitive gray jay peers from a larch grove perch in Banff's Valley of the Ten Peaks. A common year-round resident in upper montane and subalpine forests, this 11-inch-long bird is also known as the Canada jay, the whiskey jack (an anglicized version of its Cree name, wiskatjon), *and the camp robber for its pilfering habits around human habitation.*

the outskirts, hotels and motels line Banff Avenue, the community's main street. Downtown is crowded with craft and souvenir shops, fast-food restaurants, and even more hotels. Tour buses rumble across the fieldstone bridge spanning the Bow River, bound for the Banff Springs Hotel. To some, this bustling activity means money and jobs. In 1990 the town of Banff generated 61 million dollars in federal taxes, more than enough to cover the cost of operating Banff, Jasper, and three other national parks in Alberta.

To others, the value of a national park cannot be measured in dollars and cents. A meaningful relationship with these islands of relative wilderness must involve more than driving parkways and buying souvenirs. "A visit to a national park should include some form of direct contact with nature," says Mike McIvor, president of a conservation group called the Bow Valley Naturalists. "We're living in a time of ecological crisis because we've removed ourselves so far from the natural world. If there's any hope for us as a species, we have to reconnect with nature, and the best place should be in a national park."

For a few days, though, I disconnected, trading hiking trails for sidewalks. I was actually in utero on my first visit to Banff, so I didn't see much. Later family vacations to this town of 7,000 in the heart of the front ranges were much more rewarding. Reliving old memories, I swayed up the slopes of Sulphur Mountain in a gondola, feasted on spectacular vistas of the Sundance, Goat, and other ranges, and stared into the unsettling amber eyes of a bighorn sheep. I descended for a soak in the 104°F waters of nearby Upper Hot Springs, wandered through the ersatz medieval corridors of the Banff Springs Hotel, visited the outstanding

Whyte Museum of the Canadian Rockies, and toured the Cave and Basin hot springs, where Canada's national park system was born in 1885.

But I was soon ready to exchange the blacktop of Banff for the backcountry of Jasper. On this return visit I hiked on the Skyline Trail through the Maligne Range southeast of Jasper townsite. With more than half of its 27-mile length above the trees, the Skyline is considered by many to be the finest route in the Canadian Rockies. Accompanying me were park naturalist Dave Pick; Dave's daughter, Lynn; and 67-year-old dynamo Roy Richards, a retired railroad conductor.

"Uncle" Roy, who has lived in Jasper all his life, loves his park's backcountry. He sets out on many of his expeditions with a trio of cronies: an Edmonton doctor with a bum leg who has to be helped over rocks and streams; a local bookkeeper with a bad back; and a Hungarian-born forester from Victoria, B.C., who speaks too softly for Roy's liking. "It must be 15, 20 years that the group's been together," said Roy. "We didn't go last year, though. Everybody's getting older."

You'd never know it from the way Roy hikes. Crumpled fishing hat pulled low over his eyes, battered backpack cinched tight, spruce walking stick in hand, Uncle Roy set off westward from Maligne Lake at a sprightly pace, leading us through a fire-succession forest of lodgepole pine and into open alpine terrain. Autumn swatches of red bearberry and yellow dwarf birch on the gray, treeless mountainsides gave the landscape the look of an old hand-tinted photograph. "I never get tired of this country," exulted Uncle Roy. "Isn't it gorgeous?"

Beyond Little Shovel Pass, the trail descended into the Snowbowl, a soggy, beautiful valley laced with streams trickling through subalpine meadows. Uncle Roy pointed with his walking stick to a stand of spruce and fir. "Over there is Shangri-la," he said. "In winter we ski in five miles from Maligne Lake Road along Jeffrey Creek and overnight down there."

Not even an afternoon squall dampened Roy's enthusiasm as the trail climbed to 7,612-foot Big Shovel Pass. The weather lifted and once more Roy was on the lookout for his "birdies," especially white-tailed ptarmigan, golden eagles, and gray-crowned rosy finches.

We overnighted just below the pass in the lee of a 1,000-foot headwall, bunking in the cabins of an outfitter friend of Dave's. Next morning a cold, blustery wind whipped up whitecaps on Curator Lake as we made a steep ascent to the Notch, a narrow pass on the southern flank of Amber Mountain. At an elevation of 8,235 feet, the Notch is the high point of the Skyline Trail and the gateway to an extraordinary stretch of mountain hiking.

For the next three miles, we walked along barren ridges that provided views of superlative mountain scenery in every direction. On our left, we gazed down at the Athabasca Valley and farther afield to Mount Edith Cavell, the Ramparts, and a sea of summits beyond in British Columbia. On our right rose the Queen Elizabeth Ranges, a nearly continuous wall of sawtooth mountains.

Winds blasted the ridgetops at gusts of up to 60 miles an hour. A golden eagle soared high above us, effortlessly riding the air currents, perhaps setting its sights on a golden-mantled ground squirrel that huddled beneath a boulder. A few hardy plants hunkered down in the desiccating winds to survive, mostly pin-cushion moss campion anchored by a tough, woody taproot as thick as a finger, and tiny willow herb, the dwarfed alpine relative of fireweed.

As we struggled to keep our footing, Uncle Roy kept pointing out the highlights of his backyard. "See down there beside the Athabasca River?" he yelled above the howling winds. "That's the Valley of the Five Lakes. We go there on mountain bikes to look for moose. It's a great place for bushwhacking, too. I love to bushwhack!"

Finally, we left the aeries of eagles and descended into the shelter of the valley below, where pikas scampered on rock slides and marmots whistled from boulders. As we passed Mount Tekarra, Uncle Roy pointed to a steep, snow-filled gully high on the side of the mountain. "When I was a kid, some friends and I slid down there one spring on our bottoms. It was very foolish, but we did it."

The trip ended with a long descent on an old fire road through forests on Signal Mountain. My "dogs" were barking, Dave's pace was slowing, and Lynn lagged far behind. And Uncle Roy? After a couple of 13-mile days, he was

Rock climber Barry Blanchard clings to the fissured face of Back of the Lake, a 330-foot-high quartzite crag at the western end of Lake Louise.

highstepping down the fire road, singing "Seventy-six Trombones" and imitating a drum major with his walking stick.

No entrepreneur is going to get rich off people like Roy Richards. His kind of outdoor recreation—hiking, cross-country skiing, birding—doesn't require fancy equipment and expensive infrastructure, employ thousands of people, or generate windfalls for government coffers. On the other hand, Roy Richards and his gimpy but game backcountry buddies seem to commune with the true spirit of this mountain wilderness. Treading lightly through Jasper and its neighboring reserves, they leave the parks unimpaired and keep their own hearts and minds forever wild and young.

*C*raving for salt brings this mountain goat down from the safety of windswept heights to a lick along Highway 16 near Jasper's eastern boundary. Goats, sheep, moose, and other northern grazers enhance diets of grasses, sedges, twigs, and bark with minerals obtained by licking sulfate-rich deposits of glacial silt and sulfurous outcrops of black shale. For goats, the need for extra minerals is most pronounced during the June molt.

PRECEDING PAGES: Head lost in the clouds, Mount Geikie wears a fresh mantle of snow. This quartzite pinnacle, one of the Ramparts framing Jasper's Tonquin Valley, stands on the British Columbia side of the Continental Divide.
FOLLOWING PAGES: September moon sets over Little Odaray Mountain in the Lake O'Hara region of Yoho National Park.

"It is magnificent"—*so translates the Stoney word* Takakkaw. *Fed by meltwater from Daly Glacier, Takakkaw Falls (above) thunders over the lip of a hanging valley, then plunges 1,246 feet to the floor of Yoho Valley. Seven Veils Falls (opposite) splashes crystal-clear mountain water on a rock face overlooking Lake O'Hara.*

FOLLOWING PAGES: Turquoise gems in an evergreen setting, Mary Lake (foreground) and Lake O'Hara sprawl at the foot of Wiwaxy Peaks in Yoho National Park.

*P*erfect reflections in the still waters of Yoho's Mary Lake repeat the beauty of subalpine larches feathered in autumn's golden needles (opposite). Bright berries dangle from the zigzag stem of aptly named twisted stalk (below). A bolete mushroom (bottom) raises a wrinkled cap above a bed of heather.

FOLLOWING PAGES: Third Vermilion Lake slumbers beneath a blanket of morning fog, seemingly a world away from nearby bustling Banff townsite. The three Vermilion Lakes provide habitat for moose, muskrat, beaver, and more than 180 kinds of birds.

*O*utfitter Barry Ferguson leads a lone pack mule along Stony Creek near the eastern boundary of Banff National Park. In the distance, the tilted limestone slabs of pyramidal 9,750-foot Mount Oliver typify the severely folded and faulted front ranges of the Canadian Rockies. Opposite: With boots and spurs hung up for the night but cowboy hats still in place, trail guides at an outfitter's backcountry camp relax after a hard day's ride.

FOLLOWING PAGES: Peyto Lake and its unspoiled setting in Banff's Mistaya Valley display the alpine beauty of Canada's Rocky Mountain parks.

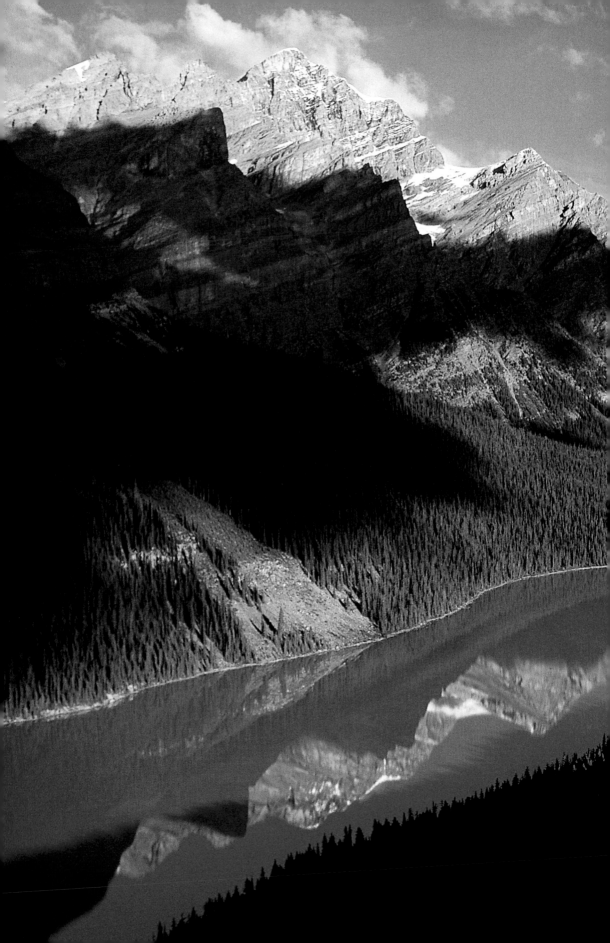

ON THE TRAIL OF
THE BISON

ON THE TRAIL OF THE BISON

by Jennifer C. Urquhart

The news from the north early in July 1954 was electrifying. A pair of whooping cranes and their chick had been spotted from a helicopter by a fire crew passing over an area of Wood Buffalo National Park in Canada's Northwest Territories. Whooping cranes were verging on extinction. Despite years of combing large expanses of northern Canada, no one had found where the last remnant wild population nested—until that fortuitous 1954 flight.

On my journey into this region, our little Cessna dipped a wing, affording a better look at the whoopers' breeding grounds. In the subarctic wilderness below spread a seemingly endless series of small, shallow ponds, ranging in color from yellowish tan to chalky white and separated by narrow fringes of spruce and pine.

Never numerous, the cranes had been overhunted as their wetland habitat shrank. During the winter of 1941-42 the regal, 5-foot-tall birds hit an all-time low, numbering only 16 at their wintering grounds at the Aransas National Wildlife Refuge on the Texas coast, 2,500 miles to the south. I could not help dwelling on a poignant picture: Year after year, the cranes, in ever dwindling, ragged skeins, beat their way northward across a whole continent to this remote place, driven by the age-old urge to reproduce. What a powerful testament to the instinct to survive!

Motionless at the center of one pond were two white dots, cranes stalking small aquatic creatures. "We were able to get close enough to see the red on the head with the unaided eye," the park biologist had reported in 1954. There would be no chance this day for us to get that close. Nor would we hear from 2,000 feet—as low as the park recommends that planes fly—the characteristic clarion call, likened by a turn-of-the-century observer to "the blast of a silver horn." It was enough to know that, with luck and cooperative Canadian-U.S. programs, the wild cranes have inched slowly back from the brink. Though their situation remains precarious, they now number more than 130.

By its very remoteness and immense size, Wood Buffalo National Park has room enough for such beleaguered wild creatures. The scale here is indeed grand. "We are going 125 miles an hour, and we are not anywhere near out of the park," the pilot on another flight had pointed out to me. Second in size in the world only

Wood Buffalo National Park in Alberta and the Northwest Territories supports vast, undisturbed stretches of grasses and sedges, prime grazing for bison. Founded in 1922 to preserve a fragment of their population, the park now shelters about 2,000 bison.

PAGES 82-3: Shaking its tail feathers and stretching its wings, a sharp-tailed grouse bows and struts in a mating ritual at Grasslands National Park in Saskatchewan. PRECEDING PAGES: Underground streams emerge at the Salt Plains in Wood Buffalo. Salt crystallizes on mudflats rimmed by saline-tolerant red samphire.

to a park in Greenland, Wood Buffalo stretches 176 miles from north to south and averages 100 miles east to west. Switzerland, or about five Yellowstones, would fit neatly within its 17,300 square miles. Largely within its boundaries lies the Peace-Athabasca Delta, one of the largest inland freshwater deltas in the world, encompassing 1,700 square miles. Following four major flyways, hundreds of thousands of migratory birds converge here at various times of the year.

It was to aid the survival of another animal that Wood Buffalo was established in 1922 by the Canadian government: the last free-ranging herd of wood bison, so named because they were considered a separate, larger, darker, northerly subspecies of the North American bison, commonly called buffalo. Though their numbers never plummeted as low as those of whooping cranes, the story of the North American bison is all the more shocking when you realize that as many as 60 million of the great, shaggy beasts once roamed the continent. In the 1880s, after the wanton slaughter—for sport, hides, meat, and other parts—as well as the cynical campaign to conquer the Plains Indian by destroying the one animal upon which his survival depended, free-ranging plains bison were all but extinct. However, 1,500 wood bison remained in what became this park.

Canada's interior plains stretch in a great arc from the U.S. border northward toward the Mackenzie Delta. The flatness of the terrain belies rich ecological diversity: Grasslands yield to pristine boreal meadow and forest, and a watery world of bog and spongy muskeg. Much of the southern prairie succumbed long ago to plow and settlement. Now Wood Buffalo and national parks such as Riding Mountain, Prince Albert, Elk Island, and more recently Grasslands, protect elements of the original diversity.

I began my journey on the trail of the bison farther south, in Manitoba. Along the way I would find many other wild creatures. Just west of Winnipeg I saw my first bison. Ironically, in this land where the real ones were destroyed, the bison was the logo on an 18-wheeler, hurtling across the featureless prairie. A whole herd followed, stamped on provincial highway signs. Ominous clouds now cast a kaleidoscope of sunshine and shadow on wheat and barley fields; the radio warned of tornadoes and advised lying in a ditch if one should encounter a twister. I checked out ditches and thought of Dorothy, of Kansas and Oz, as I sped toward a hazy blue rise at the horizon—the sheltering ramparts of the long, low upland known as Riding Mountain.

Bison once took refuge there, too. For native herds—gone since the 1870s—it was too late, and for the grizzly and woodland caribou as well, when in 1930 the Canadian government declared Riding Mountain a national park to protect what habitat and native animals remained.

"A jewel on the prairie is what this park is for me," explained senior park official Celes Davar at park headquarters in Wasagaming near Clear Lake. "The single most important thing here is the incredible diversity of wildlife: 160 species of nesting birds, and carnivores such as wolves and coyotes."

The density of wildlife is remarkable as well. In the park's 1,150 square miles flourish some 3,500 elk, and as many moose. You are likely to see some of the perhaps 1,000 black bears and the innumerable beavers. More than 650 streams and nearly 2,000 lakes and ponds water a biological crossroads. Diverse habitats of mixed hardwoods, typical of the East, mingle with rough fescue prairie, boreal spruce forest, and aspen parklands.

The area near Clear Lake, where 30,000 people may congregate in season, seems largely a bustling lakeside resort. It is different in the western reaches, in Birdtail Valley.

"This has got to be one of the best kept secrets in Manitoba, or Canada," rancher Ray Armbruster told me as we rode across his pasture and into the park where he and his wife, Susan, run horse-pack trips. It's no secret, but rarely does Ray encounter anyone here.

Riding Mountain acquired its name long ago, in the days when horseback was the preferred mode of transport across these rugged highlands. Getting into that spirit on a balmy summer day, I climbed aboard Stormy, assured that the bay gelding acquired his name through the coincidence of having been born during a raging storm. The trail cut through dense stands of aspens; then we wended our way through lush little meadows and wooded areas, where delicate columbines and vivid orange prairie lilies bloomed. We forded several streams.

The ecology has been changing. The rough fescue prairie grasses—important for deer and elk—are dwindling as woody shrubs and trees spread. Originally fire helped keep down the growth; in droughts, every 10 or 15 years, prairie fires would sweep through. Roads and other barriers now prevent that process.

The once nearly extirpated beavers, reintroduced in the 1950s, have been busy. Drowned trees rose spectrally out of several ponds we passed. The industrious rodents have become controversial as well. In damming streams within the park to form ponds for their lodges, they sometimes cause floods outside the park. Local landowners object and assert that beavers are messing up elk habitat. New studies draw the opposite conclusion, however. The beaver actually creates important habitats, certainly wetlands for waterfowl, but also meadows for elk and other ungulates. Sedges we saw in moist meadows in Birdtail Valley are the first plants to recolonize an empty beaver pond. For elk, sedge shoots provide accessible food beneath snow—critical winter habitat.

Drained beaver ponds also act as a kind of seed bank. When the water runs out of a pond, the bottom is exposed. A study of one such pond revealed seeds of 95 species of vascular plants—ones not common in the park. Many of these seeds need bare soil, which is available in the empty ponds, to regenerate.

Late in the afternoon we rode into camp along Gunn Creek, a tributary of Birdtail Creek. That evening I drifted to sleep to the rhythm of heavy rain on my tent. We awoke to a brilliant, clear morning and set out to explore the area.

From a grassy ridge, dotted with starlike white anemones and a galaxy of other wildflowers, we looked down on Gunn Creek, winding in sweeping curves. A hawk shrieked as we continued along a wide valley. The wind had freshened, riffling silvery aspen leaves, and dark clouds were rolling in. We had dismounted on a high, grassy area, the Birdtail Bench, at lunchtime, when the first lightning flickered. The bolts struck at a distance at first, then close. My horse, Stormy, danced and skittered as I stroked his neck. Now lightning and rolling thunder came almost simultaneously in a splendid light show.

Some see the park as an island of wilderness lapped by a sea of intensely cultivated farmland. Eons ago this escarpment was an island in a literal sense—an upland surrounded by the vast ancient Lake Agassiz. Higher areas of the park still reveal beach ridges left as the lake receded several times.

"It always was a kind of island situation," said park warden Wybo Vanderschuit, "higher than the surrounding prairie." With increased agricultural development, the demarcation of the park's boundaries on a NASA satellite image become even more obvious. Scientists fear wildlife populations cannot survive

S*treams of shimmering light from the aurora borealis illuminate the dark heavens
above a solitary tepee in Wood Buffalo National Park. Displays of northern lights occur
regularly here from late summer through late winter. Wood Buffalo,
Canada's largest park, encompasses 17,300 square miles of boreal wilderness
astride the border between Alberta and the Northwest Territories.
Eerily aglow in warm sunlight, a bleached bison skull (opposite) serves as
mute testimony to the ageless cycles of life and death in the park's remote reaches.*

long in an environment so separated from genetic renewal and habitat expansion.

Encounters between large wild animals and people in such island situations can be disastrous—usually for the animals. When an elk or a moose wanders out of the park it is one thing. Wolves are another. They tend to wander far, and some people still think the only good wolf is a dead one, a warden told me. Hunters take an estimated six or eight adult timber wolves each year—10 percent of the park's total. Bears, too, face problems.

"I'm going to show you that the interface between farm and park is direct," said another park warden, Pat Rousseau. Early one evening I joined the stocky, mustachioed French-Canadian on patrol. We drove through a changing medley of oak and ash, boggy areas, and dark, boreal spruce forest to the 1,200-foot escarpment at the park's eastern edge. There we gazed out onto fields of grain and yellow canola, brilliant in the fading sunlight.

"This is the islandness," said Pat. "A bear doesn't understand that the park boundary line is right here. He goes out to feed, and the farmer doesn't like it."

It's great habitat for bears, the 13-year veteran of the park told me, as he pointed out branches of a berry bush pulled down by bears, anthills that they'd dug up, and oaks from which they'd soon get acorns. Along a park road we spotted a bear, with a red tag in her ear, digging ants to eat. "That's Culvert," he said. "I've known her all her life. When she was two years old and abandoned by her mother, she lived in the culvert up here. This is her territory. She has two cubs."

The next bear, however, Pat was not happy to see. "Green Tag. I just moved her and her two cubs to Laurier, about 60 miles away, four days ago. This is a straight campground bear. She learned it a long time ago." Pat traps such bears and relocates them. He has a thick file on Green Tag, spanning three years. "The problem with garbage bears," he explained, "is that moving them as adults is hardly ever successful." Bears rove as adolescents, he explained; then they fix on a territory. "When I first moved here, in 1982, we had to put down anywhere from 20 to 30 bears some years," he said. "With improved garbage handling and education, we now average maybe one bear or two. To me it is a total failure when I have to destroy a bear. I really don't like doing it."

Green Tag had had many chances. "She's on the list now," he said. "I'll leave her alone unless she comes into the townsite. If she stays out here by the road, that's fine." Later while we drank coffee, a call came in on Pat's radio. Green Tag was in a campground. Pat had to go. I never found out what happened.

Now I turned northward to Wood Buffalo National Park. The huge park spills over Alberta's northern border into the Northwest Territories, embracing vast tracts of northern prairie and boreal forest atop the Alberta Plateau. Countless potholes, ponds, lakes, and meandering streams punctuate the largely roadless expanse. At first everything looks the same. There are no awesome mountain fastnesses or spectacular precipices. Terrain goes beyond flatness; in places it

The Bennett Dam causes the Peace River to freeze at a higher elevation in the valley. Then when spring breakup occurs, the river's ice cover can withstand a greater volume of water flow beneath it, tending to make the ice jams occur less frequently. Climate change is also instrumental in reducing ice jams. The drawdown in the fall is important too, because it exposes mudflats for migrating waterfowl. Now the drawdown is far less marked, and the mudflats have shrunk.

Later that day I trudged slowly through the grasses and thistles to observe the researchers. In places where once I might have gone swimming the hydrology crews were finding groundwater nearly six feet beneath the surface. Kevin and his crew moved slowly along a transect and took random samples of plants, recording species and frequency of occurrence. Two weather stations recorded rates of evaporation. By gathering such baseline data the crews hope to assess changes in water levels and vegetation. There are no clear answers yet. Experiments have already been undertaken with artificial ice dams to replicate seasonal flooding.

I had still not seen a herd of bison in this their last truly wild home. Moving northward to Fort Smith, I continued my search. Along the road to Peace Point, I encountered a lone bull, eyeball-to-baleful-eyeball, separated by the comforting barrier of an auto hood. The bull wallowed in the dust, heaving to the edge of his ungainly hump, then rolling back, snorting all the while. He then slowly rose onto disproportionately dainty hooves and slipped silently into the forest with a grace unexpected in a beast so large.

"Keep quiet," advised outfitter Jacques van Pelt optimistically. "Keep downwind, so as not to panic the lead bull."

Early one morning I set out with Rolf Kasting, a young German visitor. We would rendezvous 11 miles away to camp with Jacques. Sandy ruts six or eight strands wide braided through the jack pines. Truly this was the interstate of bison trails. Surely we would find them on this path they have followed for decades to reach the salt flats. They'd been here. That was clear. Thousands of them over time. The trail was gouged deep. And they'd left evidence: tufts of coarse, dark hair caught on small branches and rough bark; skulls and bones. Even fresh prints this day and newly deposited scat. Maybe a big fellow with a sense of humor was teasing us, staying one step ahead, or behind. All day long, so far no bison.

Other park creatures were not so shy. Though I was clad in a net jacket, with hood and mask, and doused in several bug concoctions, a cloud of mosquitoes trailed me, along with tenacious deerflies—aptly called "bulldogs."

I was in good company: 18th-century explorer Alexander Mackenzie endured equal misery. "A terror to man and beast," turn-of-the-century naturalist Ernest Thompson Seton waxed eloquent as he devoted a whole chapter to the little critters in his account of his 1907 journey here. Driven to distraction, in one instance he counted 30 mosquitoes in a small patch of his tent, then extrapolated that number to 24,000! My net armor foiled all but those with particularly penetrating proboscises.

The trail skirted sinkholes, where the underlying karst terrain had collapsed as water dissolved soft gypsum bedrock. Some sinkholes cradled lush vegetation. Water filled others to form ponds. At the edge of one pond a clear, fresh wolf track joined those of our evasive bison.

In the late afternoon we eased down the rocky escarpment and set out across the flats, frosted with salt where subterranean springs have spilled out. A crimson plant called red samphire, low-lying and salt-tolerant, streaked the monochromatic scene in vivid tones. Beyond islands of spruce we found Jacques and camp at the edge of a swift, cold saltwater creek.

The next morning an eerie scene greeted us, wintry-looking as if a cold fog had crept over a snow-dusted terrain. But the summer air was warm and muggy. And quiet, except for the whining of insects and the distracted shriek of a lone gull. A smoky haze had stalled over the flats, dispelling all sense of scale. More wishful than realistic, we fantasized far-off boulders as bison.

Hiking out later, we rested on a grassy knoll; a pair of sandhill cranes stalked within a few feet, calling companionably to each other in rattling, guttural tones.

We never did find bison on that trip. The next day, however, I saw close-up the source of the haze. I flew in a helicopter with fire warden Doug Walker and a crew to monitor fires. A huge bull moose took off from one pond in a galumphing gait as we flew over. Only from the air can you really see nature's tapestry at Wood Buffalo: In an intricate brocade, swaths of shrubs and trees, varying in height and in shades of green, curved around swales of meadow and muskeg bog; lakes and serpentine rivers embroidered the whole. "That's why they call it the boreal forest mosaic," said one of the crew. It is a mosaic created by a cosmic dance of fire and water and constantly changing.

Fire—usually lightning ignited—is the key factor, strangely enough, in this poorly drained, watery domain. "All trees are the same height," Doug observed, looking below us. "It's a sure sign that fire has burned an area. That's how the boreal forest has evolved," he added. In recent years, at Wood Buffalo and many other reserves, Parks Canada has realized the importance of fire to ecology and habitat variation. Except where they threaten human safety or habitation or cross park boundaries into other jurisdictions, conflagrations are allowed to run their course.

Hot weather and little rain had made this a bad fire year. We surveyed charred areas at fire number 22, almost burned out after a month—and after scorching more than 70,000 acres. Crews were now battling fire number 40, about 75 miles west of Fort Smith, because it approached the Alberta border. Doug had evacuated firefighters the evening before. "Last night it just took off," Doug said. "We were sitting in camp just finishing supper. We could hear the fire, like rolling thunder, before we could see it and thought the helicopter was coming back."

By reading the landscape, crews can predict a fire's movement. Doug pointed out white lichens, called reindeer moss, on the ground. "It indicates a dry area. Fire will creep through that." Pines and black spruces also burn easily. More moist, the aspens seem to resist all but the most intense fires.

As we neared fire number 40, Doug noticed that it had jumped the aspens. "And it's going to torch the spruces," he said. "This is not bad. Yesterday there was a 60-foot wall of flame here." Now we started to circle the fire. Warden Mike Etches activated the Global Positioning System, which uses constant satellite signals to plot exact position readings—to "draw" the fire's parameters for a computer at headquarters. "Right now we could use a lot of wind shifts," Mike said. "It just keeps the fire spinning around."

The chopper banked low, and we peered into a yawning inferno. Flames shot from the tops of already engulfed spruces and pines. "I'd sure like to see some snow," Doug said, only half in jest, as we headed back to Fort Smith.

In my wanderings I learned that even here at Wood Buffalo, a park set up expressly for them, bison are having problems. In the 1920s the park became embroiled in controversy when about 6,500 plains bison—which had outgrown their southern range and many of which had been exposed to bovine tuberculosis and brucellosis—were moved here. They soon interbred with the less numerous wood bison. The park's bison population surged to nearly 12,000.

As that number has declined in recent years to about 2,000, theories have proliferated as to why. Natural cycles may be at play: unusually deep snow cover or wolf predation. A major flood in 1974 drowned some 3,000 bison. Another theory targets disease as the culprit. Some people have speculated that vegetation changes accompanying the drying of the delta may be affecting bison habitat. Or perhaps the bison simply are going back to historical levels, before introduced herds ballooned the population.

Solutions range from doing nothing to the most draconian proposal—slaughtering all of the park's bison because they are considered genetically inferior and diseased and replacing them with so-called pure strains of wood bison from an isolated part of the park. (Aside from the absurdity of trying to hunt down every last bison in such a vast area, this proposal has aroused great public outcry.)

DNA comparisons now indicate that plains and wood bison are genetically the same. Recent studies may disprove the role of disease. All the bison in the park test positive for various diseases at about the same rate. Yet calf mortality south of the Peace River exceeds fivefold that to the north. The explanation may lie in the wolf-bison, predator-prey relationship and the character of the habitat, assistant chief warden George Mercer told me. South of the Peace, large herds concentrate in sprawling, open meadows. A wolf pack can hang around and work the herd. The habitat farther north is patchy forest, with small meadows. "Wolves might encounter a bison herd and get one calf there," he explained. Then the bison will disperse into the bush. Next time the wolf may come across a moose. "There is a greater chance that the wolves will use other prey species."

The day before I left Wood Buffalo, Métis hunter and trapper Earl Evans showed me around the park one last time. Late in the afternoon we headed back to town. Long rays of sunlight mottled birches and aspens in the forest, obscuring the shadowy shapes that moved among the trees. But the low, rumbling roar was unmistakable. At last, there they were, a herd of bison, 30 or 40 of them. Calves cavorted, and bulls jostled cows and each other. I watched, mesmerized.

It was a shock, flying southward, to see again the land carved up: farms in great geometric blocks, roads at rigid right angles, defining ownership. What a wonderful sense there is at Wood Buffalo of what was before: space and limitless freedom at the edge of civilization; wild creatures and the aboriginal peoples who have lived in close alliance with them for centuries. Only a road to its edges, then nothing. Not nothing really, but something wonderful in this vastness, where animals roam unfenced and wild birds flock by the thousand. Not just bison. Maybe this is what I had come to find.

When I was in Fort Chip, I had admired Joe Vermillion's moccasins—light brown, with dark fur trim and beaded flowers. His mother had made them, he told me, and yes, I could ask her to make some for me. After quickly tracing my foot on a piece of paper, I forgot all about them—until the package arrived weeks later, and I opened the box. The pungent smell of smoldering spruce wood—used to cure moose hide for the lovely beaded moccasins—overwhelmed the room. I was back at Wood Buffalo. The air would be chilled there by now, with spruce logs crackling in woodstoves. Moccasined feet would soon squeak-crunch through dry snow. And I would remember as I padded through my house in my moccasins.

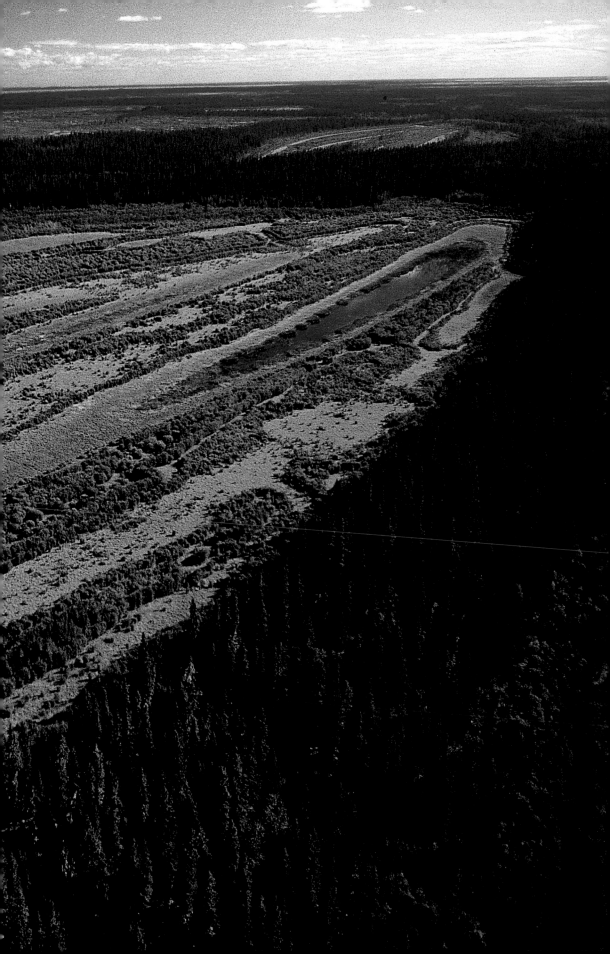

*T*all grasses all but hide a resting bison in Wood Buffalo. In recent years,
the bison population in the delta has declined, perhaps because of drying conditions,
range deterioration, and the elimination of wolf control.

PRECEDING PAGES: Marking periods of drying and flooding, varying shades of green
stripe a perched basin—a kind of wetland common to the Peace-Athabasca Delta.

*A*ppearing tiny as ants in an aerial view, bison graze on a green sward of the Peace-Athabasca Delta, a maze of marshes, meadows, shrubs, streams, and ponds. Located at the southeastern end of the park, the Peace-Athabasca ranks as one of the world's largest freshwater deltas. It serves as the resting area or breeding ground for more than 400,000 migrating waterfowl that touch down here every fall and spring. Spring also marks the arrival of whooping cranes (right), an endangered species. Their only natural nesting site in the world lies in a northern wetland area of the park. Thanks to intensive conservation efforts over the last 50 years, the whooper population here has increased from a scant 16 to more than 130. But the ultimate survival of this regal bird still hangs in the balance.

THOMAS D. MANGELSEN / IMAGES OF NATURE

*W*ild and wind-tossed, a patch of Calamagrostis canadensis, *or bluejoint reedgrass, colors the prairie landscape of Wood Buffalo National Park. Many species of grasses flourish in the park's diverse habitats.*

*A*t Grasslands National Park, a remnant of mixed-grass prairie survives, providing plenty of space for a pair of graceful pronghorns to run (above). Speed distinguishes this grasslands denizen, which can bound distances of 20 feet in a single leap and attain speeds of 70 miles an hour. With the plowing-under of the North American prairies, the populations of pronghorns suffered a serious decline. Today, the park serves as a haven for several hundred of these deerlike animals.

On the lookout, a black-tailed prairie dog (left) peers over the entrance to its burrow at Grasslands National Park. Over the past century or so, prairie dogs were nearly wiped out by farmers, who poisoned large numbers of them. Still considered rare, prairie dogs survive in Frenchman River Valley at the park's western end—the only area in Canada harboring colonies of these sociable rodents.

FOLLOWING PAGES: From a vantage atop 70 Mile Butte, a scattering of low-lying mesas presents a stark contrast to a springtime hillside softly ablaze with yellow locoweed in Grasslands National Park.

PARKLANDS NEAR
AT HAND

provided an uncommon cure for explorer Jacques Cartier and his scurvy-plagued men in 1534. Local Indians recommended boiling cedar fronds into a tea. The afflicted men drank the brew and recovered; on his return Cartier introduced *Thuja* to Europe, where it became known as *arbor vitae,* the tree of life. Two centuries later, the British Navy's use of limes and lemons to battle scurvy earned English sailors the lasting sobriquet "limeys." Using similar logic, says Doug, "the French should've been called 'cedars.'"

Unlike the majestic trees Cartier saw, the incredibly twisted dwarf before us has absolutely no soil, Doug stresses, just rock. Scotty and I stare and ponder, showing appropriate states of awe. Doug, never short on breath or metaphors, soon breaks the silence. "I would love to be that tree. It's like a big old amoeba, tenacious yet placid. It doesn't know how to quit. Let's grow over here a few hundred years. Stop. Now grow over there."

Among flatland trees, size often equates with survival: Crowd out neighbors and grab the sun. But grow big on a cliff, and you soon exceed the tensile strength of the rock; the cliff fractures, and you fall. Better to grow slowly or not at all, like fish in an aquarium or bonzai trees in tiny pots. Consequently, growth rings of cliffbound cedars are so narrow and dense that a microscope is needed to tell where one ends and the next begins. But such trees actually live far longer than they would if rooted on soil-rich flats.

*S*hipwrecks—almost two dozen of them—stud Fathom Five's depths, drawing a steady stream of sport divers, snorkelers, and tourists in glass-bottomed boats. The schooner Sweepstakes *(opposite) has spent a century just below the surface of Big Tub harbor, while steamer W. L. Wetmore (right) lies off Russell Island.*

"It makes you ask, what is success?" says Doug. "Here these little guys are living through the equivalent of five or six generations of the other, musclebound cedars. The relationship between size and age is almost inverse."

He tells me of an especially memorable find. "It was dead, but very recently dead, because it still had leaves and a cone. It weighed 11 grams—less than half an ounce—the whole tree! It was about the size of a fork, its cross section no thicker than a pencil. And it had 155 rings. That's less than a tenth of a gram per year, for an entire tree for its whole life. And it still had babies! If there is a maximalist thinking in society, there must be a corresponding minimalist thinking somewhere, and this has got to be it."

*N*amed for its urnlike shape, a rocky "flowerpot" towers about 40 feet above Georgian
Bay's azure waters, at the edge of Flowerpot Island in Fathom Five National Marine Park.
Such natural stacks result largely from uptilt, erosion, and the presence of hard caprock
atop softer shales and limestones. Similar structure underlies other offshore islands
as well as Bruce Peninsula itself, all part of a major geologic feature known as the Niagara
Escarpment. Cobbles and boulders (opposite, top) pave many Fathom Five beaches,
while fissures in the platelike surface rock shelter a wealth of wildflowers, from harebells
to these balsam-leaf ragworts (opposite, bottom).

He estimates that the diminutive "God" before us is 800 years old—maybe much more—and could live another 600 or 700 years. Another cliffbound cedar on the Bruce had more than 1,650 rings, making *Thuja* the oldest tree species in eastern North America (California's bristlecone pines and redwoods are older), and the slowest growing woody plant known anywhere. Its vertical realm, Doug contends, comprises an ancient and virginal forest that is distinct from horizontal ones—even the peninsula's—because it includes 10 or 15 additional species that occur only here, on the cliff face.

"The cliff has a sense to it," he adds, "a predictable assemblage of species that do predictable things. For me that's what makes the definition of a forest. It's so

Playground for the adventurous, Bruce Peninsula's Georgian Bay coast offers a rugged and crannied counterpart to the park's flat Lake Huron shore. "The Grotto" (left) lures swimmers with two underwater connections to the bay. Nearby parapets overlooking deep inshore waters draw cliff-top divers —and spectators (opposite).

compact. Grotesque, but serene." And able, somehow, to survive. The cliff's porous rock drains away rainfall, creating a "limestone desert." Its steepness keeps it bare of protective snow in winter, when temperatures plunge to minus 35°F. "Here's a habitat," he says, "that gets blasted in winter, pounded by waves, then baked by the sun in the summertime. It's the closest thing to Arctic tundra there is around here, and nothing should be able to grow there. Anything that does, gets my respect. In a way, what we're doing is not much different from exploring a new planet. These cliffs are places that nobody has ever studied, that no one has ever wanted. They've been left alone for 10,000 years. And I find that really, really cool. I know I overuse that scientific term. But show me where else in the world you can find a pristine, presettlement forest in the middle of millions of people. Southern Ontario is steel mills and farms and industries and highways and little knickknack shops and stuff. Not virgin forests. That's what everyone thought."

What amuses Doug most about this odd little forest is that its oldest known tree sample was found beneath a park sign warning people to stay out of a cave.

"It was a tree that had died and apparently fallen off the cliff and been covered by a rockfall. Parks personnel cut it because it was in the way of where they wanted to put the sign. Isn't that a hoot? We had it dated, and it goes back to King Tutankhamun, 1350 B.C.! Imagine, here in the middle of southern Ontario there's part of a tree that's been sitting around waiting for somebody to pick it up since the time of King Tut; now *that* is cool."

About 300 miles northwest of Tobermory lies Ontario's biggest, wildest, and remotest national park: Pukaskwa, wedged between the Trans-Canada Highway and Lake Superior's northern shore. It includes some 725 square miles of rugged, spare backcountry. Apart from paved access to a headquarters and campground near Hattie Cove, it is totally without roads. A single major hiking trail parallels the Superior shore for nearly 40 miles. Several lakes and close to a dozen small rivers fret the park. Only two are navigable; one offers white and the other flat water for those able to organize their own logistics. Except for Hattie Cove, Pukaskwa tends to draw hard-core hikers, canoeists, and kayakers. Its rolling, rounded profile rises no more than 2,080 feet above Superior's often foggy surface.

Boreal forests—composed mostly of jack pine, aspen, black spruce, and white birch—blanket the land, thinly. Wolf and black bear still roam here, as do moose and a few woodland caribou. Beaver, lynx, and fox are common, having recovered from man's past trapping excesses.

Superior, of course, is voyageur country, crisscrossed for hundreds of years by explorers and traders and priests and trappers—and by Indians for thousands of years before that. More recent human activities include logging, both for timber and pulp. Giant booms made up at Pukaskwa and other Superior logging camps were routinely towed to Sault Ste. Marie as lately as 1965. Even today, a local pulp mill and several mining operations continue to exploit resources just outside the park. This land may not be pristine, yet it remains inarguably enduring, and somehow primeval—at the very least, feral—in feel. Its exposed bedrock is pure Canadian Shield, a mix of ancient basalts and granites and other igneous and metamorphic rocks, the youngest of which have lasted well over half a billion years. They have been smoothed and sculptured by time and countless glaciers, ground down but by no means conquered.

Naturalist and Harvard professor Louis Agassiz visited what would become Pukaskwa National Park in 1848, but even he did not dare far inland—thanks to daunting hordes of blackflies. He was moved, however, by the area's awesome sense of permanence. "A heavy stillness seemed to hang over [the land] and weigh down every sound," he wrote. "It was as if no noise had been heard here since the woods grew, and all Nature seemed sunk in a dead, dreamless sleep."

The same feel embraces the park today. Its interior lakes, difficult of access, drip with solitude. Superior's rounded, buttressed, and often fog-drenched shore offers stark beauty but few comforts—or secure harborages—for passing boaters. The hills and coast retain a chilling aloofness. Time has proved them marginal places for human habitation. Now, with the park's creation, they will remain so.

Like Pukaskwa, southern Quebec's La Mauricie National Park consists of rolling and rounded Canadian Shield rock, up to a billion years old: the lake-dappled Laurentian Mountains. Its terrain and spaces are less daunting, however; they seem warmer, more soothing to the human soul. Its forests—like those of Bruce Peninsula—blend northern and southern species. A loop road provides varied views and access to this park's interior. Truly near at hand, La Mauricie sits midway between Montreal and Quebec City, a couple of hours from either. It is thoroughly recreational in outlook, drawing visitors four seasons a year.

Chief Warden Thierry Bouin sums up his park's attractions: "It's a gentle, friendly, comfortable environment. The mountains are not huge. There's wildlife, but none of it is dangerous. You can drink the water right out of the lakes. There are all kinds of opportunities for recreation, things like canoeing, biking, picnicking. Fall is spectacular because of the forest colors, the maples and birches. Summers are warm. Winters are not too cold, but cold enough to do some good winter activities. Lots of snow, so we have a long season for cross-country skiing. We maintain about 80 kilometers [50 miles] of groomed trails."

Chief Naturalist Jacques Pleau adds that, even though he spends most working days out in the park, he often chooses to vacation in La Mauricie as well. "I'll go to one of the lakes, go camping, hiking, and often there's hardly anyone there. It's like it belongs to me. That's the feeling you get here."

Indeed, senior Parks Canada personnel so prize this park's scenery—and its proximity to city services and conveniences—that they rarely pass up a chance to transfer here. An adage among them says it all: "When you get to La Mauricie, you die at La Mauricie." Quite a compliment for an area known in the early 19th century simply as "The Wasteland."

La Mauricie's name stems from one Maurice Poulin de la Fontaine, a 17th-century fiscal officer and owner of nearby lands whose other accomplishments seem to have escaped the history books. No matter. By the mid-20th century, much of the present-day parkland had been split among 20 or so fish-and-game clubs, including the exclusive Laurentian Club, founded in 1886. Members avidly hunted bear, moose, and deer, and netted trout—but their enthusiasm for the outdoors also encouraged most clubs to be sound conservators of the land and its wildlife. Even so, the fact that these reserves were closed to the public (including local, largely French-speaking residents), while club memberships favored Canada's largely Anglophile, ruling elite sparked resentment among some Quebecois. Today, the park stresses an egalitarian approach. Access is open; camping and other facilities are situated to provide visitors maximum use without destroying the character of the land. Again and again, I would marvel at the design of its trails and picnic spots, even the exceptional carpentry of its boardwalks.

"Our facilities," Jacques assured me, "are second to none." Thierry agreed: "We do things large and solid and heavy-duty. They're overdesigned to provide better environmental protection. We make boardwalks—not because we don't want people to get their nice hiking boots all dirty—but because we know that with the number of people that are going to walk a trail, if we don't provide a boardwalk, they will enlarge and enlarge the trail, and eventually we'll end up with something that is totally unaesthetic, trampled."

While the park has a number of interpretive walks and easy hiking paths, most trails here are portages connecting different lakes. By emphasizing portages rather than, say, lake-encircling trails, the park accomplishes two things: It avoids wear and tear on lake shorelines, and encourages canoeing, a favorite regional activity. For countless centuries, canoeing—not tramping the forested hills—was the way to get around. La Mauricie, in fact, lies near the heart of Quebec's canoe-manufacturing industry. Local makers now use fiberglass or cedar or even Kevlar, but shun the heavier plastics preferred for whitewater use. This park's small but numerous lakes make canoeing synonymous with portaging, and so local canoes are lightweight, equally at home on open waters or forest walkways.

La Mauricie claims some 150 lakes, more than any other of Quebec's four national parks, and each has its own personality. Wapizagonke, a big finger lake, is the heart of the park; it claims the largest campground (219 sites) and draws the most visitors. Park employees often favor Anticagamac, near the park's western edge, partly for its relative isolation and partly for its variety, which ranges from sheer cliffs and brash, bouldered waterfalls to a marsh that draws waterfowl and moose. Lac du Caribou boasts sparklingly clear waters and sandy beaches. Lac Bouchard, partly drowned by a recent beaver dam, is a boggy affair walled in by cedar, spruce, and paper birch. Lac Gabet lies just far enough off a loop road—about a mile—to exude an extra sense of seclusion; it harbors loons and some of the park's biggest maple, birch, and beech trees. Rock-browed Lac du Fou, split into several major lobes, has water so dark and tannin-stained you'll have trouble seeing not only its bottom, but even the end of your canoe paddle. A narrow neck of water connects it to Lac Besace, where boulders stud one shore, while marsh grasses line another.

While La Mauricie is relatively small and heavily used, its terrain subdivides it into so many valleys, bowls, lakes, nooks, and crannies that many visitors can find solitude here, all at the same time. Most lakes can't be seen from other lakes. Many, in fact, can't be seen very well from shore. Trails often end right at a lake, without exploring any shoreline. The result is that you need a canoe to experience La Mauricie fully.

I visit this park in early October. Autumn assaults the senses: The flaming reds of maples, the buttery, golden birches, and the spicy perfume of balsam fir set the mood. Loons call. The air is frosty, the sky a brilliant blue, the firs so green they seem edible. Indian summer is a good time to canoe, free of crowds—though breezes may come up. Time it right, and you can drift effortlessly down Wapizagonke, using your back as a mainsail, your paddle as rudder. Take in the undulating Laurentians, glorious in the season's foliage. Today's scenery may seem eternal, but actually is very recent. La Mauricie's billion-year-old bedrock greatly predates trees of any sort; when it first took shape, life was primitive, restricted to the oceans. Then—and long after—erosion here ran rampant, unmitigated by any greenery. Unfathomable ages passed before towering mountains of ice blanketed this land, abrading its mighty peaks into today's hills. Conifers colonized La Mauricie only 8,000 or 9,000 years ago; maples and other hardwoods followed a couple of millennia later.

Walking the trails and canoeing the lakes, I see great blue herons, mergansers, and ruffed grouse. In Wapizagonke, what seems at first a swimming moose turns out to be a black bear. I hear again the outrageous song of the loon, ironic in that this particular lake draws so much human traffic that the birds no longer nest here. Yet they are here now, and...who knows? Other sounds come to ear—the rustling chorus of aspen and birch leaves, the slap of a beaver tail. A hawk flaps and wheels, alighting in the top of an old pine. Ducks burst from one watery hideout to splash down in another, their wings whistling squeakily overhead. In a natural amphitheater near Lac Gabet, fall colors still blaze, but from the forest floor rather than the treetops; winds have displaced the leaves. Naked branches thinly veil distant views of the bare-knuckled Laurentians. Suddenly the faint, mournful honking of geese causes me to stop and search the graying sky. High up, 80 or 90 birds wing south in a big, ragged V. The same breeze that has blown all day now seems a touch icier; clearly, Indian summer's glory is past. Time for some creatures to leave, for others to stockpile berries, nuts, other fodder. Moose and bear and deer will linger yet. But I, like the geese, must move on.

*T*otems of the good life crowd the docks at Beausoleil Island in Georgian Bay Islands National Park, reflecting the growing challenge of balancing high human use with the welfare of rare residents such as the spotted turtle and Eastern massasauga rattlesnake.

PRECEDING PAGES: A lighthouse on tiny Brebeuf Island, close by much larger Beausoleil, marks a stretch of the main shipping channel to the port city of Midland, Ontario. FOLLOWING PAGES: Sculptured by glaciers, buttressed with moraines, flooded by ice melt, Georgian Bay's eastern edge boasts about 30,000 islands and innumerable coves. This meeting place of land and water draws almost 200,000 boaters yearly.

*A*long Lake Superior's northern shore, Pukaskwa National Park promises outdoor enthusiasts some of the wildest terrain in any of Canada's near-at-hand parks. Summer attractions include the White River's falls (opposite) and far less daunting streams, as well as thousands of acres of untracked forest and more than 100 miles of frontage on North America's inland sea. One recent July 1st, Canada Day celebrations prompted volunteers to don voyageur garb and tote a traditional birchbark canoe (above).

*N*orth woods sonata: Wood lilies (opposite), a snapping turtle, and a bunchberry in bloom provide a triplet of natural grace notes near Pukaskwa's Hattie Cove area. The same site also draws most of the park's visitors, for it harbors the headquarters and interpretive center, as well as campgrounds, hiking trails, and access to Superior's shore.

FOLLOWING PAGES: Autumn's calico forests frame Wapizagonke, largest of the 150 lakes dappling La Mauricie, amid Quebec's worn and rolling Laurentian Mountains.

ATLANTIC
OUTPOSTS

ATLANTIC OUTPOSTS

by Cynthia Russ Ramsay

Scudding clouds cast fleeting shadows on the orange-brown landscape before me—a barren sprawl of rock incongruously close to a forest dense with evergreen trees. There was reason to expect such curious scenery, for I was in Newfoundland's Gros Morne National Park, an untamed realm of nearly 700 square miles abounding in geologic wonders that have earned the park designation by UNESCO as a world heritage site.

My journey would also take me from the western coast of Newfoundland south to another island preserve—Nova Scotia's Cape Breton Highlands National Park, where the mountains meet the sea in a sequence of dramatic headlands separated by secluded beaches. In both parks wilderness occasionally gives way to a scattering of fishing hamlets along the coast. But people seem like intruders in the bogs lush with berries and in the highland plateaus patterned with miniature flowers and stunted forests. In addition to these unspoiled attractions, Gros Morne National Park showcases rare and remarkable rock formations that draw geologists and other visitors from all over the world. To those who can read the rocks, the park's terrain offers dramatic testimony to changes in sea level, glaciation and weathering, the collision of continents, earthquakes, and volcanic eruptions in the depths of a now vanished sea.

For the people who live along Gros Morne's 45 miles of coast on the Gulf of St. Lawrence, fishing rather than geology is the main focus. Today these tight-knit communities mourn the days when fishing for cod was the mainstay of the economy and a way of life. Establishment of the park in 1973 has brought income from summer tourists, but unemployment due to the declining fishery still sends many young people away. Sentiment often brings them back.

The hamlets exist as enclaves within the park. The residents have special privileges such as the right to harvest wood from designated areas. Though old ways are dying, the people still retain something of their traditional, subsistence lifestyle—hunting hares, moose, and caribou (outside park boundaries), cutting firewood, planting vegetables, raising a few sheep, and catching fish.

One of these self-reliant Newfoundlanders is Clem J. Reid, Gros Morne's lanky

Pruned by wind, ice, and salt spray, conifers along the coast in Newfoundland's Gros Morne National Park form dense tangles known locally as tuckamore. The stunted conifer forests also grow in Nova Scotia's Cape Breton Highlands National Park.

PAGES 138-9: The scenic Cabot Trail winds along three sides of Cape Breton Highlands National Park, offering visitors dramatic seascapes.
PRECEDING PAGES: Wild breakers in the Gulf of St. Lawrence explode into spray against rocky outcrops off Presqu'île, a headland on Cape Breton's rugged west coast.

backcountry specialist. Born 32 years ago in Norris Point, a fishing village on Bonne Bay, Clem is a man with the quiet, contained manner that comes from living by one's hands and wits.

"I can feed myself and get along without a whole lot of cash outlay. It's a satisfying lifestyle as long as you enjoy working with your hands and have a sense of humor. You also have to understand you're never going to own a BMW," said Clem, as we set out on the James Callaghan Trail to the top of Gros Morne, the 2,644-foot mountain that gave its name to the park.

Its French name has been anglicized so that the "s" is pronounced. The words, which mean "big knoll," can also be translated "big gloomy." And it is, as Clem observed, "a hard-looking piece of property." From a distance the mountain's stony bulk, rounded by age and smoothed by ice, rose above the surrounding forest like the humpback of some giant, slumbering beast. Nearer, we could see the steep expanse of talus on its southern face.

From the trailhead we started out across land that had been logged, providing a second-growth forest of alder and birch a temporary place in the sun. But the trail soon led us into a classic boreal forest of black spruce, white birch, and balsam fir. The trees, particularly the scrawny black spruce, bore the stamp of their hardscrabble existence in a land of scant soil and long, harsh winters. Because black spruce tends to shed the needles on its lower limbs as it grows, many of the trees look like giant bottle brushes. "It's a self-pruning process that concentrates the chlorophyll where it does the most good," explained Clem.

Some spruces were whiskered with pale gray-green lichens that hung in tendrils from the branches and trunks. Called old-man's beard, the lichens added a spectral touch to these northern conifers.

Higher up, where the shadowy forest gave way to broader vistas, we took the Ferry Gulch section of the trail, which cut through a dense tangle of stunted trees—black and white spruce, balsam fir, mountain alder, and white birch— known locally as tuckamore. Nature's bonsai nipped by wind, ice, and salt spray, tuckamore fills in the dips and hollows, where there is some protection from the weather. There's no way to tell whether it's ten inches or ten feet to the ground beneath the tangle of contorted trees.

From a cliff at the edge of the flat-topped mountain the land suddenly fell away to Ten Mile Pond, a long lake with remarkably deep, clear water set against gray cliffs rouged in places with shades of pink and red. We could see the rolling plateau of the Long Range Mountains, the northernmost remnant of the Appalachians. But the vista flaunted no peaks.

Over millions of years, erosion carried away the high contours and left a nearly featureless peneplain, which was subsequently uplifted and sculptured by glaciers into a landscape of low ridges mottled with bogs and ponds. Apart from the infamous tuckamore, the land holds neither forests nor heights. Nothing intrudes upon the great, all-encompassing dome of the sky.

"It's a place where you have the world to yourself," said Clem, with a hint of sentiment in his voice. "But it's rough country. In summer the blackflies are more vicious than the weather, which is forever unpredictable. You can be stranded for days waiting for low clouds to lift. There are no landmarks, so unless you use a compass, you can get lost pretty easily. There aren't any trails except for the paths worn by the caribou." About a thousand woodland caribou, close kin of the barren-ground caribou, spend most of the summer up on the Long Range. "They're easy to find in June and July, because they herd up on the snow beds to get away from the clouds of insects," Clem explained. "But some males go their own way, probably because the females don't want them around until the rutting season in the fall."

We encountered one of these solitary stags on Gros Morne's summit plateau. He paused, perhaps to check us out. His curiosity kept him in place for a minute or two, but then he trotted away with his head held high. For me, this wild creature of the north, with his white cape and long, sharp-tipped antlers, symbolizes the unspoiled wilderness that is the soul of the park.

We walked across the summit bent against a wind that tugged at my jacket and brought tears to my eyes. Looking down, however, was a distinct advantage in a landscape where the tallest objects were waist-high cairns marking the trail for times of near-zero visibility. Ground-hugging tundra plants took root in the thin, gritty soil between the rocks. Crowberry's needlelike leaves formed dense green mats. Sedges, tundra dwarf birch, and partridgeberry had also found a home, creating a thin layer of life on this time-altered remnant of an ancient beach. Originally the quartzite had been sand deposited close to the shores of the Iapetus Ocean, a proto-Atlantic that separated North America from Europe and Africa 600 million years ago.

Few places, however, can bring into focus the changing character of the earth's surface and the inconceivable measures of geologic time with better clarity than the Tablelands. The most important geologic feature of the park, the Tablelands offers a rare look at mantle rock. "Until the late 1960s no one guessed how such a deep-seated rock had come to lie on the surface of the Tablelands," said Douglas R. Grant, a scientist with the Geological Survey of Canada who has spent more than 20 years studying the geology of Newfoundland. "We knew it was very dense rock coming from miles below the planet's crust. The explanation had to wait until the concepts of continental drift and plate tectonics made sense of it all."

About 570 million years ago the continents on either side of the Iapetus Ocean began to move together. Far out to sea, the edge of the North American plate slipped under the Eurasian plate and was dragged down toward the mantle. Big slabs of rock, like ice floes, were pushed westward against the edge of North America, and the land buckled like a rumpled rug. Oceanic crust and mantle rock lay stranded on top of continental shelf rock in the center of Pangaea, the supercontinent formed by the united landmasses. In time the continents began to separate again, and a new ocean, the Atlantic, grew between them.

On a guided walk, park interpreter Robert Hingston explained why the terrain was so barren. "Mantle rock has a peculiar chemistry with relatively high amounts of metals such as nickel and chromium and toxic concentrations of magnesium, which discourage most plant life. It's also lacking nutrients that plants need, such as nitrogen, potassium, and calcium," Rob told a group of visitors as we followed him along the base of this queer mountain.

Close-up, we could see it was not entirely naked. Scattered here and there were a great variety of plants growing low to the ground, including an uncommon number of carnivorous plants. The secret of their success is that they draw nourishment not only from the soil but also from the insects they snare.

"Sundews and butterworts trap their prey with stickiness—like flypaper," Rob said. The more flamboyant pitcher plant—Newfoundland's provincial flower—has a different method. Insects lured onto the reddish cup-shaped leaf will slip from the slick, waxy lip into the "pitcher," which is half full of rainwater. Inside the leaf, tiny hairs point downward, preventing prey from crawling out.

"Living within this rainwater are bacteria, larvae of one species of mosquito, and numerous other small organisms that act as the stomach of the plant, helping it digest its prey," Rob explained, using an eyedropper to suck up some of the plant's liquid.

Among the noncarnivorous plants able to tolerate the magnesium-laden soil is the shrubby cinquefoil. Found all over the Tablelands, its bright yellow buttercup-like flowers are seen throughout the summer. Moss campion copes by creating its own soil. It grows in tight, round clusters over a thick batting of its own dead

*L*ow tide exposes algae and tidal flats around a glacier-quarried boulder in Bonne Bay (left), a fjord that cuts deeply into Gros Morne National Park. Cloud shadows dapple slopes of the 2,644-foot peak that gave the park its name. Moving ice sculptured the 2,000-foot cliffs (opposite) of Western Brook Pond, a majestic landlocked fjord traversed by sight-seeing boats in the summer.

leaves. "One of the best recyclers," said Rob, gently probing a clump to show how deep the cushion was.

I spent a morning in the woods a couple of miles east of the Tablelands tagging along with Carson Wentzell as he checked snares baited to capture black bears. If an animal is caught, Carson calls park wardens, who tranquilize and fit it with a radio collar. When the bear is released, signals from the collar allow scientists to track its movements and provide data on the habits of these powerful beasts. Here they may weigh up to 600 pounds, and they have a reputation for being particularly active predators of young moose and caribou.

"They live mostly on roots, berries, and carrion, but these bears can also take down an adult caribou," said Carson, as we headed toward the first of nine snares.

"In most cases bears avoid people, if they hear or smell them coming." Carson walked ahead warily, carrying a shotgun because inspecting snares is not without risks. "If a cub is in the snare, an angry mother will be waiting right there."

Though there was bear scat in front of it, the snare was empty. Still, a bear might be foraging nearby. We listened for snapping branches or rustling leaves, but heard nothing except the black-capped chickadees, tiny birds with large voices chirping in a cheerful staccato.

I peered inside the twiggy tepee that housed the snare and formed a single, narrow route to the bait. Sharp sticks were set upright around ursine delicacies—

pieces of road-killed moose and doughnuts dipped in molasses. If a bear went after the feast, there was only one soft spot to put a paw. Covered with moss, it concealed a pressure paddle that would fire a loop cable and clamp around a leg without injuring the animal.

"If the bear steps only partly on the wire, he doesn't get caught," said Carson, spraying a mixture of vanilla and butterscotch extracts around the site. "They say the bears can smell this stuff for five miles."

But the bears were finding something else more tempting. Or perhaps they were just pretty smart, for the ninth snare was as empty as all the others.

The Viking Trail, Newfoundland Highway 430, passes park headquarters near

Rocky Harbour and runs along the East Arm of Bonne Bay, a masterpiece of glacial landscaping. Carved by ice and then flooded by the sea, the bay has two probing arms that reach far inland and divide the park into a northern section and a smaller, southern one. In summer Bonne Bay is a haven for small, open boats that once could barely contain their loads of cod.

The area around the bay has a human history spanning millennia. From about 2500 B.C. a succession of peoples—the Maritime Archaic Indians, the Groswater and Dorset Paleo-Eskimos, and a recent Indian culture— camped, hunted, and fished in these environs. About A.D. 1000 the Vikings established a settlement at L'Anse aux Meadows some 200 miles to the north, and they may have sailed south along Newfoundland's west coast. But until French explorer Jacques Cartier made his first voyage there in the summer of 1534, the west coast remained uncharted.

Although the French established a presence on Newfoundland, the island was ceded to Great Britain in 1713 with the signing of the Treaty of Utrecht. France, however, retained fishing rights along part of the coast, which came to be known as the French Shore. In 1783 the Treaty of Versailles changed the terminal points of the French Shore to include the entire west coast.

By the terms of the treaty no permanent settlements were allowed in this area, but it wasn't long before transient Englishmen who caught salmon, herring, and cod in summer began wintering over. By 1904, when France traded away its rights in Newfoundland waters, there were permanent fishing communities that also made trapping and canning lobsters part of their business.

After the turn of the century, logging became an extra source of income for many fishermen, who swapped nets and lobster pots in winter for axes. But the small-scale, inshore fishery was the essence of their existence. And in

*R*ock *heaved up from the earth's interior forms the Tablelands (above), geologic wonder of Gros Morne National Park. Some 490 million years ago a collision of continental plates thrust a huge slab of oceanic crust and underlying mantle rock called peridotite onto the surface of the earth. Water moving through cracks in the peridotite altered its chemistry, creating veins of green, scale-patterned serpentinite (opposite, lower right); pyroxene crystals cover the surface of peridotite (opposite, lower left). The mineral composition of mantle rock discourages most plant life, but yellow blossoms of shrubby cinquefoil, grey wool moss, and blue harebells add touches of color on a drizzly day.*

Newfoundland the word "fish" means cod. Today, however, the cod population has collapsed, and the government has banned cod fishing.

Carl Rumbolt remembers when the 18-foot, open boats almost foundered under the weight of the catch. I met Carl, a sturdy, soft-spoken retired fisherman, at the park's Broom Point exhibit, where a refurbished fish store and cabin help tell the story of how it was when local people made a living from the sea.

"We'd go out two times a day, weather permitting, and use dip nets to scoop the fish out of the cod traps," he said, showing me a net box 60 feet square. "These traps were used in summer, when capelin come to shore to spawn. Big schools of cod would follow them right into the opening in the trap." Carl explained that the

*W*hen lobstermen have lifted the last pot of the season, their neatly stacked traps and orange gloves accent the clapboard architecture at a fishing camp near one of the coastal communities within Gros Morne.

small, smelt-like capelin could swim out of the trap, but not the cod. Later in the season the men fished with a gill net or a handline.

Carl's six sons all had a go at fishing. "But they didn't hang around very long; the work was too hard. I didn't mind the labor. Problem was you didn't get paid for it," said Carl. "Back in 1960 a fish with its head off and guts out was 2½ cents a pound, but it sold on the mainland for 50 cents a pound. Now you'd get 36 or 38 cents with the head on. But there are no fish."

Carl also remembers when the only transportation was by water. It took years for the road to get to Broom Point, where the Mudge family fished each summer from 1941 to 1975.

"They'd come down by boat from Norris Point, bringing hens along for fresh eggs," Carl related as we walked over to the small cabin where the three Mudge brothers and their wives had spent each fishing season, from April until the end of August. The cabin has been restored and furnished in the style of the mid-1960s. Missing from the cabin, with its kerosene lamps and battery radio, is a boiling tea "kittle," a stew pot bubbling with salt cod, potatoes, onions, and fried salt pork "scrunchons," and the bustle that had made the small place home. Here the women cleaned, salted, and dried the cod in the sun, baked bread in the wood cookstove, and did the wash in the gas-powered machine with a hand wringer.

A scattering of similar frame houses, with slatted lobster traps piled in front, defines Sally's Cove, smallest of the park's village enclaves. Its buildings were larger in size than the Mudge cabin, but were built to the same uncomplicated, boxy specifications that make the architecture as straightforward as the people.

On the following day a heavy overcast sky threatened rain as Clem Reid and I set out from park headquarters to take a cruise on Western Brook Pond, a modest name for a major landmark. In Newfoundland any body of fresh water, except for the very largest, is called a pond. Gros Morne's most dramatic pond is a glacially cut, freshwater fjord ten miles long and hemmed in by granite walls. At one time it was open to the Gulf of St. Lawrence. But as the glaciers melted, land that had been weighted down by ice rose some 300 feet above present sea level, exposing a narrow coastal lowland that blocks the gorge from the gulf.

From Rocky Harbour we drove nearly 17 miles north on Highway 430 to the 2-mile trail leading to the tour-boat dock. The park has built boardwalks across boggy areas that are remarkable for what lies beneath the surface. A thin layer of plants grows on top of dead, waterlogged vegetation that has been piling up for 8,000 years. Clem explained that bog water is cold, acidic, and contains almost no oxygen, so there's no decay. "Stems and leaves just become pickled into peat."

At first Clem thought we might encounter moose, for they like the open wetlands. But some people were out in the bog, picking berries—amber-colored relatives of the raspberry known locally as bakeapples. "So the moose were drove," Clem remarked in his understated way.

Instead of wildlife, we came upon the glories of a landscape carved and polished by glaciers. From the pond shore, looking across two miles of open water, we could see the towering cliffs bracketing the mouth of the gorge, a deep and dramatic notch in the Long Range Mountains. Glaciers and erosion had done the work. A V-shaped river valley had been transformed into a steep-sided canyon eight miles long with the distinctive U shape that is the signature of moving ice.

As the tour boat with 20 passengers on board entered the mouth of the gorge, the ramparts towered 2,000 feet above us, their lines so sharply cut they seemed to have been split by some cosmic cleaver.

"A lot of stiff necks go out of this place," Clem said. He pointed toward a slender waterfall spilling smoothly through a cleft in the rock for hundreds of feet. Other falls looked like silvery tassels hanging on great slabs of stone. As we moved through the sinuous gorge, a marvelous creation of pale granite and dark water, I contemplated once again the mind-wrenching magnitudes that shape and reshape the earth. Eternities of winter and forces of unfathomable power have created the landscapes of Gros Morne National Park.

Fierce winds like those that pummel Gros Morne, capricious weather, and long, hard winters also characterize Cape Breton Highlands National Park on the northern end of Nova Scotia's Cape Breton Island. The sky there changes like a kaleidoscope, and storms that arise with sudden fury have swallowed ships without a trace or swept their cargoes up on the shore. At Chéticamp, an Acadian fishing village near the western gateway to the park, the year 1874 is remembered as *"L'année de la farine"* because of the flour that floated ashore; another year, a storm produced a "butter summer." And 1931 was merrier because smugglers had to jettison a cargo of rum.

The August day was balmy, and skies were unfailingly blue when I drove from Chéticamp, on the gulf, to Ingonish Beach, the park's entrance on the Atlantic coast. The drive of 65 miles covers one of the most scenic sections of the 180-mile Cabot Trail. Named for John Cabot, a navigator who sailed under the banner of England and may have landed on Cape Breton Island in 1497, the roller-coaster highway winds around all but the southern edge of the park. From the heights, cars look like toys, and the highway offers vistas of timbered valleys and crescent beaches set between granite cliffs that provide perches for bald eagles. The eagles wait there, swiveling their white heads like spectators at a tennis match, as they scan the sea.

More than 25 hiking trails, from half a mile to 16 miles long, take off from the park's section of the Cabot Trail. I followed a number of them to wooded glens laced with waterfalls, to lakes rippled by black ducks, and to steep headlands that seemed cantilevered above the water.

"The Cabot Trail exposes you to about 10 percent of the park. The rest is a vast interior wilderness with boreal forests and highland barrens," said David Lawley, an amiable naturalist who knows all the great spots for picnics and the quiet places where you can hear the sad, eerie call of loons.

Like most visitors, we drove the Trail, stopping along the way. First we hiked to the crest at Presqu'île, a headland with an appropriate French name meaning "almost an island." Unrelenting winds had produced an alpine tundra at sea level, with miniature purple asters, tiny white spires of yarrow, and patches of crowberry—all species inured to hard times. Seaside plantains, looking like tiny green starfish, hugged the ground beside pale blue harebells nodding in the wind on stems a few inches high.

Another trail led to the Grand Anse Valley, where stately sugar maples and red oaks made us feel like midgets as we strolled across the ferny ground. "All eastern North America once looked like this," said David with a wave of the hand that took in a dozen towering giants, each spaced about 20 feet apart. At the edge of this splendid old-growth forest, which becomes more splendid with the colors of fall, we came to a sheep crofter's hut with thick stone walls and a roof thatched with rushes, called Lone Shieling. A replica of a humble cottage once common in the Scottish Highlands, it was built in 1942 to meet the terms of an earlier land grant that gave the park its start. This little bit of Scotland reflects Cape Breton's strong Highland ties. When lairds evicted thousands of tenant farmers from their lands in the early 19th century to make way for more profitable sheep, many Scots landed here, settling according to their place of origin—those from Inverness in one place, those of Barra in another.

For lunch we returned to Chéticamp, where the accent is Acadian with a 17th-century flavor. The ancestors of the inhabitants were French settlers who came to Acadia, today's Nova Scotia. Victims of the 18th-century conflicts between the British and French in Canada, the Acadians were deported in the mid-1700s—an ordeal immortalized in the poem *Evangeline* by Longfellow. But after the long struggle ended, some Acadians came back to Cape Breton Island. Thirteen families had settled in Chéticamp by 1790, and most of the names in the telephone book today belong to descendants of those returning exiles.

The community has preserved a strong sense of its Acadian identity and customs. But when it comes to music, Acadians enjoy Scottish, Irish, and country-and-western tunes as well as their own. Fiddler Donnie LeBlanc was playing a lively Highland piece when I joined the jovial, beer-drinking crowd at the regular Saturday matinee at the Doryman. Down the street Le Gabriel also served up toe-tapping rhythms that drew groups of friends and relatives from villages along the coast.

Before the day was over, I went on a whale-watching tour aboard an excursion boat piloted by Gilles Chiasson, a slight, dapper figure who has turned to "fishing for tourists ever since the cod industry collapsed." Just after we left Chéticamp's harbor, sleek, jet-black shapes broke the surface of the water. Conspicuous bulbous foreheads identified them as pilot whales, a toothed species that feeds on squid.

"Fishermen would follow pilot whales because that's where we'd find herring, capelin, and mackerel—fish that are the squid's favorite food," Gilles told me in his softly accented English. Pilot whales are also known for their urge to follow a leader and their devotion to companions; if one becomes stranded, its distress cries may bring others to shore. We saw dozens of these mammals, rolling like porpoises through the swells with barely a ripple, as the setting sun cast a streak of gold upon the dark, shiny water.

I spent the night in the park's lap of luxury, the elegant Keltic Lodge near Ingonish. The white, gabled building rises majestically above sweeping lawns, manicured gardens, and a golf course famed for its vistas and challenges. "The golf course is a big revenue producer for the local communities, though the park just about breaks even operating it," said Dave Algar, an enthusiastic backcountry and communications specialist.

Tall, angular, and athletic, Dave revels in Cape Breton's winter, with its annual snowfall of about 15 feet along the coast and much more in the interior. "When the snow is down, you can go everywhere on skis," said Dave. The park's 25 miles of groomed, cross-country ski trails lead into valleys, where the dark rivers turn silver with ice, along the coast, where the sea is frozen white, and into the immense, flat, interior wilderness of the barrens.

A short drive on the dirt road to Paquette Lake took us to the only easily accessible corner of the barrens, the park's tundra wilderness. We stepped onto a seemingly boundless plain of far horizons. Although the ground was carpeted in a muted composition of lichens and heath plants, the great, open expanse was overwhelming in its emptiness. Patches of reindeer moss, a lichen resembling a bit of crumpled gray paper, provided the background to a tapestry in green, broken here and there by clumps of black spruce jutting from the hollows.

As we picked a path dictated by the ripening blueberries, Dave turned to me and said, "In a few weeks these barrens will explode with color. The larches turn gold, and the blueberry leaves go bright red. In autumn this place looks like a tartan shop."

At the time I was more impressed with the bounty that was staining my hands purple. But even as I relished the sweetness of my harvest, I felt the daunting loneliness of that raw vastness of space at the bottom of the sky. "Here in the barrens you're in the weather," said Dave. "Except for the odd bird and occasional moose, what you see is the sky."

A moose can be six feet tall at the shoulder, but the year-old bull I encountered was smaller. As I moved closer, Dave warned, "Watch out if the ears go back. It means you're bothering him." I was trying to get a closer look at the way moose feed, for they have unusual dexterity with their bulky upper lip. Dave explained, "Moose don't have any top front teeth—like hockey players."

Our destination after lunch was the top of 1,200-foot Franey Mountain. We followed a footpath bordered with dwarf dogwoods, or bunchberries, each cluster conspicuous for the shiny red berries at its center. At the summit we had another look at the park's spectacular mix of landscapes—a panorama that puts people and time in perspective. In a voice warmed by enthusiasm, Dave said, "When feeling small doesn't matter anymore, you have something to remember Cape Breton with."

In a meadow bounded by rugged cliffs and the Gulf of St. Lawrence, sheep graze the lush slopes at Green Gardens on Gros Morne National Park's southwest shore. Abundant rainfall along Newfoundland's west coast nourishes forests, bogs, meadows, and wildflowers such as the showy lady's slipper (below).

PRECEDING PAGES: Cloud-filtered sunset silhouettes a boat on the sheltered waters of Bonne Bay. Residents fish, grow their own vegetables, and cut firewood from designated harvest blocks in the park.

Normally solitary, three bull moose (below) feed together at a MacKenzie Mountain pond in Cape Breton Highlands National Park. During the fall mating season moose become more social as they gather to breed. Two bulls spar with their antlers (opposite) in a test of strength. Occasional roadside visitors, moose prefer the boreal highlands that lie just beyond the Cabot Trail. By the early 1900s moose had disappeared from Cape Breton Island because of overhunting and disease; but in 1947 and 1948 they were successfully reintroduced into the park, using animals from Alberta.

*A*utumn's alchemy flames a red maple leaf and gilds ferns on Franey Mountain
in Cape Breton Highlands National Park.

FOLLOWING PAGES: Creating a flamboyant mosaic, frost and dwindling daylight turn
larches yellow and blueberry bushes red on the highland plateau near Paquette Lake.

HERITAGE OF
THE NORTH

HERITAGE OF THE NORTH

by Jeff Rennicke

"Nothing," Lawrence Kayotuk says, passing the binoculars back to me. All morning we've been perched on the edge of a ridge in Ivvavik National Park, methodically searching the scenery unfurling beyond our feet. It is a classic Arctic landscape—treeless and open, shimmering with light, constellations of wildflowers blooming next to patches of snow that have lingered into July. Across the valley, through air as clear as new ice, the British Mountains look close enough for us to touch with just an outstretched finger. On their flanks, cloud shadows the size of islands drift in the ocean of space.

Ivvavik is one of the wildest national parks in Canada. There are no RV hookups, no scenic turnouts. The nearest all-weather road ends more than 120 miles from the park. It is a wild place defined by the curves of its own horizons. Here, the only lines are grizzly tracks on the riverbanks. In this park there is still the chance of topping a rise to find a tundra pond ruffled by the wings of thousands of snow geese or to watch a herd of musk oxen sweep across a delta like runaway dust mops. But what we are looking for from our ridgetop are the barren-ground caribou.

I know they are out there. Once, on another trip to the park, we awoke in tents pitched on this very hillside to the spectacle of caribou flowing down the slope toward the Firth River. We watched a hundred animals, mostly females with calves, splash into the current, sprays of water kicked up by their hooves lit into diamonds by the low sun.

That group was but a trickle in the flood of caribou that migrate through the park twice a year, spring and fall. The Porcupine Caribou Herd—some 152,000 animals—winters in the mountains south of the park near the Porcupine River. In April, with snow often still deep in the trees, the pregnant cows start to move first, trudging northward through the mountains to the calving grounds. They are joined later by the bulls, juveniles, and barren females.

If the spring sun is strong and no late storms slow them down, the caribou move right through the park to one of the core calving grounds near the coast, centered on the Jago River drainage in Alaska's Arctic National Wildlife Refuge.

Rafters come safely through rapids near Sheep Creek on the Firth River, the main access for the few hundred annual visitors to Ivvavik National Park. Among Canada's oldest rivers, the 105-mile-long Firth flows through the British Mountains to the Beaufort Sea.

PAGES 164-5: Bathed by the warm light of dawn, 6,596-foot Mount Asgard towers over Turner Glacier in Baffin Island's Auyuittuq National Park, "the land that never melts." PRECEDING PAGES: Milling around a tundra pond in Ivvavik National Park, part of the 152,000-animal Porcupine Caribou Herd nears the end of the annual fall migration.

But if the snows stay deep on the coastal plain, calving takes place in the foothills west of the Babbage River; tens of thousands of females, all calving, turn the park into a huge birthing ground. It is this event that gives what was once called Northern Yukon National Park its present name: Ivvavik, which means in the Inuvialuit language, "a place for giving birth to and raising young; a nursery."

"Nothing," Lawrence says it again as if he can't quite believe it and takes the binoculars back for another look. It is mid-July. The caribou should be trickling back, herding up for the push south as the first stars of autumn begin to pierce the long blue sky of summer. Like most people who come to Ivvavik, I am here to witness the passage of the caribou. It is one of the great symbols of the Arctic, a pulsing of life that flows through this land as powerfully and as insistently as the Firth River. This time of year, up every valley and across every hillside, there is the possibility of life, the possibility of caribou.

"Caribou steaks, caribou stew, caribou burgers…." Over dinner at a camp near Joe Creek, Lawrence Kayotuk is reciting a list of his favorite foods. "What's your first thought when you see a caribou?" I ask him. "Supper," he says, smiling. "If I'm not hungry, I can see their beauty as animals too," he adds later, "but it is hard when so much of what you've eaten in your life comes from caribou."

Lawrence is an Inuvialuk from Aklavik, a village about 125 miles from the park, and a trainee boatman with Canadian River Expeditions, which is outfitting our trip. It was Canada's settlement with the Inuvialuit (the Inuit of the western Arctic) that created the 3,926-square-mile Ivvavik National Park in 1984, the first national park designated from a comprehensive native lands claim. Lawrence, like many Inuvialuit, thinks of Ivvavik as his park. After dropping out of school in the seventh grade, he ran a trapline with his father for several years over a route that took him far up into the park. He knows this country and, he says, there is something on the ridge he wants me to see.

Lawrence sends me off with a few vague directions and a final "you can't miss it." Of course, I do, walking right past to another ridge before turning back. Then, in a different angle of the light, I see it clearly: 12 flat stones laid in a crude circle just below the top of the ridge. A tent ring.

Ivvavik, archaeologists say, may be among the earliest inhabited regions of North America, peopled by hunters following game across the Bering land bridge. For 10,000 years the Thule and earlier peoples, Mackenzie Eskimos, Inuvialuit, and other Inuit have hunted on the Yukon North Slope, their lives closely entwined with the lives of sea mammals, fish, birds, and, most of all, caribou. Perhaps a thousand years ago a hunter set up his skin tent on this very spot for an open view of Joe Creek. Then he waited, listening to the tent flapping in the wind, scanning the distance, hoping for the slightest hint of movement on the great, still land.

But the circle of stones is not just an ancient artifact. It is a link in a chain of life on the land that continues to this day. Under the legislation creating the park, the Inuvialuit retain exclusive rights to hunt in Ivvavik. "It is very important to us to be able to harvest the caribou, musk ox, beluga whale, arctic char," Joey Amos, an Inuvialuit hunter and member of the Inuvik Hunters and Trappers Committee, told me. In part, that importance stems from a simple physical reality. The harsh climate of the Arctic makes farming impossible. Groceries must be trucked or flown in from far to the south, making them scarce and expensive. "Too expensive," says Amos. "For what I'd spend on groceries for just my family I could go out and do a good hunt for maybe three or four families."

But it is more than just money. "We hunt to eat, sure," Amos says, "but we also hunt because it is our way, our tradition, our life." The implements of that life have changed—rifles, outboards, and snowmobiles instead of harpoons, kayaks, and dogsleds. Still, the Inuvialuit hunting tradition continues on a seasonal rhythm that echoes through the ages like a drumbeat: "ratting" for muskrats in early spring; hunting caribou in the spring and fall, beluga whales in the summer, and ducks and geese in the fall. At various times of the year, they take advantage of the runs of certain fish, such as whitefish, cisco (herring), and arctic char.

Inuvialuit annually harvest more than 30 different species of animals and plants. The family diet in the six Inuvialuit communities consists of as much as 65 percent "country food," food that, by tradition, is shared; a gift of dried cisco handed across the decks of two boats, a meal of caribou heart in a tent at a remote hunting camp, a box of blueberries left on a doorstep. "There's no such thing as 'my caribou' or 'my whale' in our culture," Amos explains. "This year I got one beluga whale. That's 15 or 20 pails of muktuk. There's no way I'm going to eat all of that, no matter how hungry I get."

"It's the same for caribou," he continues. "When I go out hunting, I'm not just doing it for myself. Sure, I want some of it, but I'm willing to share with others. And if I run short of something myself, I know they will return the favor in kind."

To some, the idea of hunting in a national park may be controversial. Not to Ivvavik National Park Superintendent Peter Lamb. "The legal aspect is very straightforward," he says. "The Inuvialuit Final Agreement states that there will be subsistence activities in the park. From a philosophical point of view, the goal of a national park is to preserve the integrity of an ecosystem. Up here people have always been a part of this ecosystem. Sometimes people look at a national park and see just critters and soil and water. We're saying here in Ivvavik that the Inuvialuit culture is a part of this ecosystem and should be allowed to continue to be a part of it."

It is a relationship that works, the Inuvialuit say. Hunting has gone on here for thousands of years, Joey Amos points out, and yet wildlife populations remain healthy and stable. If the wildlife is threatened by anything, they say, it is by oil and gas exploration, road building, development, and problems brought in by outsiders, not by traditional subsistence activities. They point proudly to the 1988 Polar Bear Management Agreement between the Inuvialuit in Canada and the Inupiat in Alaska to protect the great white bears of the Beaufort Sea. They point to the councils and committees that oversee harvesting rights and help co-manage the park. And they point to unwritten laws passed down from hunter to hunter for generations—never take a beluga with young, always let the first small band of caribou pass so that the main herd will follow their migration route, treat every creature with respect. "Take only what you need and use all that you take. That's the way I was taught," Joey Amos says.

If all of this makes them sound like conservationists, it is all right with Andy Carpenter of the Inuvialuit Game Council. "Conservation, to us, means long-term protection of our land and its resources," he says, "so that we can continue to depend upon them for our food and our way of life. Conservation means thinking of our children so that they can have the same option as we do for living off the land." It is a way of life older than national parks, older even than the ring of rocks above Joe Creek where so long ago a hunter sat patiently scanning the hillsides.

One thirty-seven in the morning. Still, some of us have not yet gone to our tents. We sit alone or in small groups, talking, reading, or just watching the

*W*hen signed on June 5, 1984, the Inuvialuit Final Agreement became the first comprehensive land claims settlement reached with an aboriginal people in northern Canada. Culminating years of negotiations between the Inuvialuit and the Canadian government, the IFA both created Ivvavik National Park and ensured the Inuvialuit a voice in their future. At a celebration marking the IFA's tenth anniversary, Elder Martha Harry (right), a drum-dancing instructor from Inuvik, and Gerry Kisoun (above), an Inuvialuit member of the Royal Canadian Mounted Police, join in festivities that included Inuvialuit songs, dances, speeches, and the traditional game of blanket toss (below).

hillsides painted shades of pink in the Arctic summer night. This far north the sun does not set from May 25 to July 15. Like a stone skipping across a tundra pond, it dips low along the horizon and then bounds back up into the sky. The long, slow dip bathes the land in a honey-colored light that picks up even the slightest hue— the blush of fireweed, a streak of orange lichen, the wisp of a fishing line as one of the guides casts for char, alone upstream.

It is this endless sun that fuels the burst of life which defines summer in the far North. The Arctic is often unfairly depicted as bleak—lifeless and barren. It is an old joke: hold up a piece of blank white paper and call it a picture of the Arctic. But summer in Ivvavik is a symphony of life. Clouds of hatching insects drift on the breeze like smoke. The tundra vibrates with birdsong; patches of fireweed and cotton grass seem to bloom before your eyes. Whole hillsides resound with the chatter of ground squirrels. It is a frenzy. It has to be; soon it will be gone.

The endless sun touches us as well. No one wants to sleep. We eat at midnight, go off for hikes at all hours, then sleep until the heat rouses us from the tents. "Inuit time," Lawrence calls it. In the villages children ride their bicycles until long after midnight; at whaling camps along the coast hunters wait for the nightly calm before setting off in their boats.

It is difficult to close your eyes to it all. I sit on a hill by the river and wonder, how do I write about this light? What names are there for the colors swirling in the water where it ripples over the shallows and then goes deep and still in pools behind the rocks?

FLIP NICKLIN

The joy of a good back scratching: Beluga whales, the most common whale in Arctic waters, use the gravel in shallow estuaries to scrape off dead skin. These white whales, up to 15 feet long and weighing more than a ton, were known as sea canaries to early sailors because of their varied repertoire of sounds.

On my first trip here I met Margaret Florence Ludwig, an oil painter from Ontario. I watched her lugging her lap-size paint box and easel up hills and across creeks, and wondered how her painter's eye perceived the light. But I hesitated to ask. Such questions are difficult to phrase. Finally, I decided to try.

"You noticed it too!" she said, stopping in mid-brushstroke. "I thought I was the only one. This afternoon on our hike everyone seemed to be looking for birds or staring at flowers while I was fascinated with the light. The mountains, did you see, were sort of coral colored and were undulating in the heat."

Even at age 65 Margaret insisted on working in the field despite the rigors. "When people work in a studio," she said, talking to me over her shoulder as she

174

painted, "they don't get the adrenaline going the same way. They don't get that excitement in their brushstrokes." She explained, brushing mosquitoes away idly with her free hand, how the snow, wind, ice, and searing sun that transform nature are the same elements she seeks in her work.

That artwork is soft, the lines between ridges and sky indistinct and thick with earth tones—fitting for this place. Ivvavik is an ancient landscape, and the Firth is one of the oldest rivers in Canada. By some climatic quirk, much of the park was not glaciated during the Ice Age. Unlike the cut-glass peaks and U-shaped valleys of glacially sculptured parks like Kluane or Auyuittuq, this is a landscape shaped by millions of years of erosion by wind, water, and frost: rounded hills, narrow side-creek canyons, and columns of rock known as tors.

Looking at Margaret's paintings, I realized how foolish it is to believe a landscape can be summed up simply by putting names to its peaks or numbers to the reach of its borders. National parks have an effect on the human spirit far beyond measure. They inspire. At the Great Northern Arts Festival, an annual event that draws nearly a hundred artists, most of them Inuit, to Inuvik in the Northwest Territories, I listened as artist after artist spoke of how the land touches their work: Myrna Button, whose stained glass and watercolors are inspired by the light she sees as she runs her dog team; Stanley Nitbuktun Felix, a carver whose subjects emerge from the legends of Inuvialuit elders; and artist-pilot Judith Currelly, who flies wildlife surveys in the Arctic. "This fragile, extraordinary land," she says, "deserves to be appreciated, respected, and valued, not just for its

material resources, but for the simple beauty and wonder of its existence."

By now, the sun is salmon-orange on the high peaks. Down by the river, a fishing line is still flicking like a thin strand of lightning out over the dark blue surface of the water.

In the morning, Lawrence is less worried about the luminous beauty of the river than about getting his raft through the next 100 yards of it unscathed. I've asked him several times upstream how he feels at the oars. "Good," he answered every time. "I can't wait to get to a big one." This is a big one. Sluice Rapid.

Guiding is another way the Inuvialuit hope the park will benefit their people. Every commercial trip is required to have an Inuvialuit guide. Lawrence, on his second trip, is warming up to the work. "I enjoy showing people my homeland. It is good for them to see it, to understand how it is up here. It is so different from where they live, with cities built right next to each other, crowds of people, all the noise." He may wish he was in one of those cities now as he nervously drifts toward the rapid.

"Don't worry," I joke with him. "If the worst happens, they'll probably rename it after you." He only grunts. Lawrence follows the lead raft, setting up nicely in the first waves, but then gets pulled too far left, careening us toward a rock the size and shape of a wrecked bus. He rows hard, the muscles in his neck stretched like ropes. Suddenly his right oar twists and is ripped from the raft. There is a moment of panic, but our momentum carries us past the rock. With one oar Lawrence guides us safely into the calm water below.

It is not pretty, but we are through safely, and the lost oar is recovered. "Not bad," I tell him as we drift. Lawrence gives no reply, his feelings hidden by his ever present dark glasses and a cloud of smoke as he draws hard on a cigarette.

By Sheep Creek, and calm water, Lawrence is more talkative. "You know, the Inuvialuit are going to run this park someday," he says as we tramp through a pouring rain to the site of the park's field station. He is right. In its management plan the park states that the predominant number of staff for Ivvavik National Park—within the park and in the district office—will be Inuvialuit. "What we are trying to create here is a community-run park," says Peter Lamb, "that could mean 100 percent Inuvialuit staff eventually."

Sheep Creek is the summer headquarters of one of those Inuvialuit employees: park warden Tyson Pertschy. Pertschy, a man Lawrence calls "brother" because he was "adopted in the heart" by his family, meets us at the door and invites us in despite the fact that we are dripping wet. He is waiting for a helicopter to take him and a crew upstream for a campsite survey and apologizes that he must continue packing while we talk.

Although he was born in Edmonton, his mother is an Inuvialuk and "the north is where my heart is, for sure," he says. He spent time on the land with his uncles, hunting and trapping. It was their influence that led him to stay in school. "They kept saying, even back then, that things were changing, that there were going to be opportunities out there for people with an education."

Early on, he was drawn to the philosophy of the park. "This park was established not just for wilderness recreation or wildlife," he says, "but also for the preservation of the Inuvialuit culture and the inherent right to use the resources of the land for as long as we can imagine time. I wanted to be a part of that."

He has been, working with this park since 1989. It is not always easy. "Sometimes I feel caught between two cultures," he says. "The Inuvialuit sometimes see me as a park employee and the park sometimes looks at me as an Inuvialuk." But both cultures have served him well. His college education has given him the scientific skills his position requires. And he has learned from the land as well. "This can be rough country," he says, gesturing toward two patched holes in a wall of the field station's main building, one from a grizzly clawing its way in and one from clawing its way out.

"Traveling with my uncles taught me values and ideals—respect for and knowledge of the land and its wildlife, and especially respect for family," Tyson explains further.

It will be some time before the idea of a community-run park becomes a reality at Ivvavik—"10 or 15 years," says Peter Lamb. Large obstacles remain.

Schools in the north have dropout rates as high as 88 percent. Alcohol abuse is high. The Inuvialuit, like many other aboriginal peoples, are struggling to maintain their traditional culture while taking on the demands of today's world. But the June 5, 1984, signing of the Inuvialuit Final Agreement—the same agreement that created the park—gave them control over a 31,585-square-mile area and a cash settlement of 170 million dollars. More important, perhaps, it gave them a voice in their future.

School kids now have the opportunity to learn languages other than French. Inuvialuktun, the Inuvialuit native language, is taught at both the elementary and secondary schools. Students take part in "on the land" programs, which help preserve the traditional ways; and throughout the Northwest Territories new curricula that reflect the philosophy of aboriginal peoples are being implemented. The park has hired a community liaison. And leaders are emerging from within. In traditional Inuvialuit culture leaders were those who knew the land, its gifts and its needs. In days past that meant hunters, trappers, and fishermen. Today it may be businessmen and teachers.

Or park wardens. Tyson Pertschy, at 27 years old, is uncomfortable with the idea of being a role model. But as I hike back to the rafts I keep thinking about the nickname given him by his Inuvialuit uncles: Anguti. Loosely translated, it means "one who is still striving to reach his potential." Maybe Tyson Pertschy is a better symbol for his Inuvialuit culture than he is ready to admit.

Where the canyon walls peel away, leaving the Firth to braid itself out across its delta, a bedrock knob rises 100 feet above the coastal plain like a wave turned to stone. Engigstciak. This landmark is among the most important archaeological sites in the western Arctic. For 10,000 years hunters from nine cultures, including every known Inuit culture, have come here looking for big game.

We've seen only two caribou since the first morning on the ridge. There have been trails etched six inches deep over empty passes, rafts of floating fur, sandbars knitted with tracks. But no caribou. It has been like chasing a parade, rounding each corner only to find that the floats have already passed and the crowds all gone home. All around us are signs that the big groups have already crossed the river, ten days, two weeks ago, it is hard to tell. But they have crossed.

And we missed it. It is a roll of the dice. Early snows, sudden cold, no one knows for sure when the caribou will move or by which route—east off the summer range back into the park, across the Firth River, and south toward the wintering grounds. They just go. There is no predicting it. All you can do is put yourself in the way and hope to get lucky.

Guide Dave Evans knows what it is like to get lucky. On another trip he found himself in the middle of a large band estimated at 30,000 animals. "It was the Fourth of July," he tells us one night along the river. "We had stopped for lunch when someone looked up at the ridge and said 'Hey, there're some caribou!' Someone else said, 'There're some more!'" Soon caribou were pouring into the river, streaming down every valley, traversing steep cliffs, clattering down every draw. "We could hear them grunting," Dave said. "It sounded like a herd of pigs."

For nearly 24 hours the caribou passed in a steady stream. Evans and his group sat on boulders surrounded by a river of caribou. "Once, about 3:30 in the morning, in all the frenzy, a wolf trotted to within 20 feet of where we were sitting before noticing us, then just walked away as if hypnotized by all the caribou."

Evans tells the tale wide-eyed, as if he'd witnessed a miracle. And I suppose he has. But it is a miracle some fear could be in danger.

In the Arctic National Wildlife Refuge, directly across the border from Ivvavik, proposals are still being considered to open a 1.5-million-acre parcel known as the "1002 lands" to oil and gas exploration. Preliminary estimates say there is a one-in-five chance of striking economically recoverable oil, which would be 3.2 billion barrels, or the equivalent of a 200-day supply at the 1988 rate of U.S. consumption. Unfortunately for the Porcupine Caribou Herd, that oil, if there is any, lies directly under the traditional calving grounds.

Full-scale development could require hundreds of miles of pipeline and roads, drilling pads, airstrips, port facilities, worker housing, and more, laid like a giant fishnet over the heart of the coastal plain that has been called America's Serengeti. A draft report by the U.S. Department of the Interior claimed that "the change in habitat availability and value, combined with increased harvest, could result in major population declines...." That could have drastic effects on some 9,000 aboriginal people in 15 communities in Alaska, the Yukon Territory, and the Northwest Territories who depend on the Porcupine Herd. "It would ruin them," says Victor Mitander, former chairman of the Porcupine Caribou Management Board. "Every aspect of their lives depends on the caribou. Their economy, their culture, their lifestyle, even their health. The caribou are the heart of their communities. People hunt caribou, eat caribou, and talk caribou. Without the caribou, they would be empty people in a dead land."

Canada has made its position very clear, setting aside both Ivvavik and Vuntut National Parks, as well as the Old Crow Flats Special Management Area, to preserve the heart of the herd's habitat on its side of the border. The Canadian government has recommended coordinating management of these areas with the Arctic Refuge to create a "Caribou Commons." It has also urged the U.S. to designate the 1002 lands as part of the National Wilderness Preservation System. Canada, and the caribou, are still waiting for an answer.

Sitting atop Engigstciak, I ask Lawrence if he can imagine Inuvialuit life without caribou. For all his patience with my questions, this is one he can't bring himself to answer. He looks at me a moment and then back out to the distance. The silence rolls out between us as endless as the tundra.

The Arctic Refuge brings into focus just how vulnerable the Arctic really is. It can seem a harsh, forbidding place, untouched and untouchable. Yet, its fragility is startling. The tracks of a single bulldozer across the tundra can take decades to heal. The disruption of even a relatively small area such as the 1002 lands can reverberate like a gunshot, affecting the survival of wildlife and humans hundreds of miles away. It is a lesson we should have learned before.

On Nunaluk Spit, a gravelly finger of land jutting into the Beaufort Sea at the park's northern boundary, we kick up chips of bone in the gravel, some small enough to fit in your hand, others as large as a ship's propeller: bowhead whale.

The 60-foot, 100-ton bowhead was one of the first Arctic resources to be exploited by outsiders. During the 1890s as many as 15 whaling ships wintered at Herschel Island off Ivvavik's coast, taking hundreds of bowheads a season. In 1892 one American ship, *Mary D. Hume*, brought home the baleen of 37 whales, a record take worth $400,000. To early British whalers, the bowhead was the "Greenland Right"—the right whale to kill since it is a slow swimmer, floats when dead, and yields more baleen and oil than most whales. A single whale's blubber could be rendered into a hundred barrels of oil for streetlamps and lubricants; its ton of baleen could be used in women's corsets and umbrella ribs.

Before commercial hunting whales were "as thick as bees" in the waters near Ivvavik. Modern estimates of the population of bowheads in the western Arctic in 1848 range from 12,000 to 21,000. By the 1935 international ban on commercial whaling of right whales, bowheads were considered among the most endangered cetaceans, with a population of some 3,000.

Depletion of the bowhead meant the loss of a highly cherished traditional food source for the Inuvialuit and the loss of a cultural activity. An even more tragic legacy was the effect of the whalers on the Inuit. Prior to contact with the whalers there were perhaps 2,000 Inuit living along the coast. By 1910 the population was estimated at just 130, devastated by epidemics of measles, influenza, smallpox, and other maladies brought in by the whalers, diseases for which the aboriginal people had no natural immunities.

Both the bowhead and the Inuit are recovering. The bowhead population in the western Arctic is roughly 7,500 animals. The Inuvialuit, with growing cultural and political strength, secured a license in 1991 to harvest a single bowhead. At 5 a.m. on September 4, 1991, at Shingle Point, east of the park, Inuvialuit hunters from Aklavik successfully landed a 36.5-foot whale, after towing it through the night under the shimmer of the northern lights. It was the first bowhead taken in Canadian waters for decades. A circle, long broken, had been renewed. "The elders," says Billy Archie, a hunter in the boat that made the first harpoon strike, "had tears in their eyes."

Endangered species, oil exploration. It is becoming increasingly obvious that the Arctic is untouchable no longer. Still, by some estimates as much as 13 percent of the world's remaining wilderness lies in Canada, much of it on lands straddling the Arctic Circle. It is the one Arctic resource we've been slow to recognize.

Even though the first Canadian national parks were set aside as early as the mid-1880s, it was nearly a hundred years before any lands above the Arctic Circle were targeted for park status. The first was Auyuittuq; plans to designate this collection of glaciers and peaks on Baffin Island a national park were announced in 1972. To date, there are just four other national parks in the Canadian Arctic— Ellesmere Island, which is Canada's second largest and among its most remote national parks; Aulavik, with its herds of shaggy musk oxen; Vuntut; and Ivvavik. Land was set aside in 1992 for a national park on north Baffin Island. A timetable for establishment of this park is included in the 1993 Nunavut Land Claims Agreement of the eastern Arctic. This agreement also calls for the creation of a Nunavut Territory. Nunavut, meaning "our land," will come into being on April 1, 1999. It will encompass one-fifth of Canada's landmass and will be governed by the Inuit. Formal proposals have been made for at least five more northern parks, some of which may be established through land claims agreements.

Slowly, we are coming to see that the Arctic is no longer beyond the reach of harm. Preservation by isolation is not enough. If the Arctic is to remain a pristine, culturally rich land we must set aside places like Ivvavik, with the goal of protecting and sustaining the land and the people for, as Tyson Pertschy would say, "as long as we can imagine time." Alone with these thoughts, walking on the coast beneath a full moon the color of old whale bones, I recall words spoken at a public planning meeting. "As long as wind blows and rivers flow," said a resident of Old Crow village, "let there be protection for Ivvavik National Park." Yes, I think to myself, turning back toward my camp on the beach. Yes.

*W*inter rules Ivvavik, with no sun from December 1 to January 10 and average monthly
temperatures above freezing only three months a year. Wolf Creek (opposite) flows
through perennial ice sheets known as aufeis. Ice chokes the Beaufort Sea (above) from
October to June. Still, willow catkins (top) herald the coming of summer.

PRECEDING PAGES: With a chorus of booms, the Firth River breaks up in June. Propelled by
the swelling river, ice hacks at riverbanks and gouges new channels across gravel bars.
In the distance, Okpioyuak Creek joins the Firth as it flows across the coastal plain to the sea.

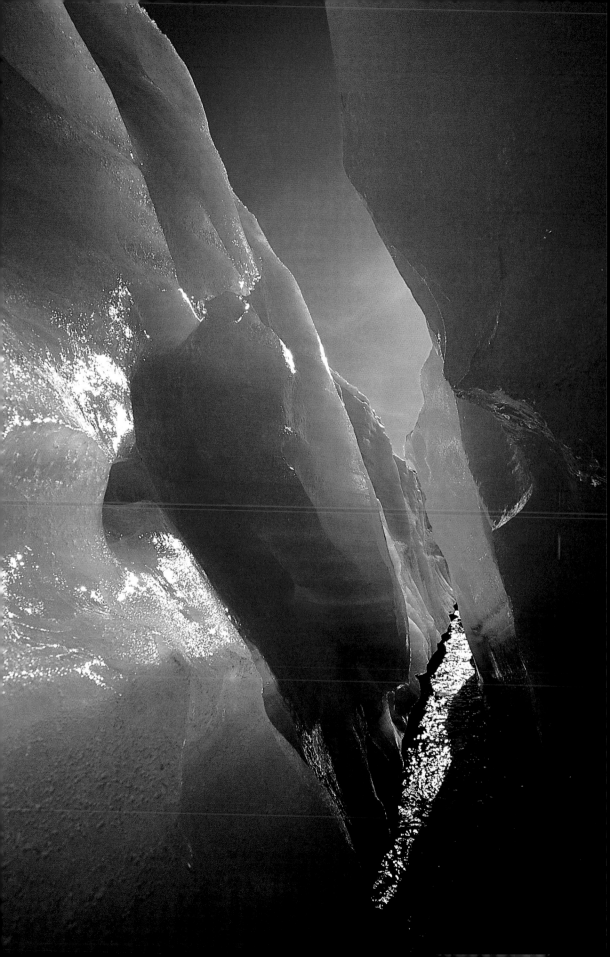

From the distant glimpse of a moose to a face-to-face encounter with a porcupine (right), the seeming emptiness of the Arctic can suddenly come to life.

FOLLOWING PAGES: To a grizzly, melting snow means the beginning of a constant search for food. With just a few months to store up enough fat to carry them through a six-month hibernation, grizzlies eat everything from caribou calves to crowberries.

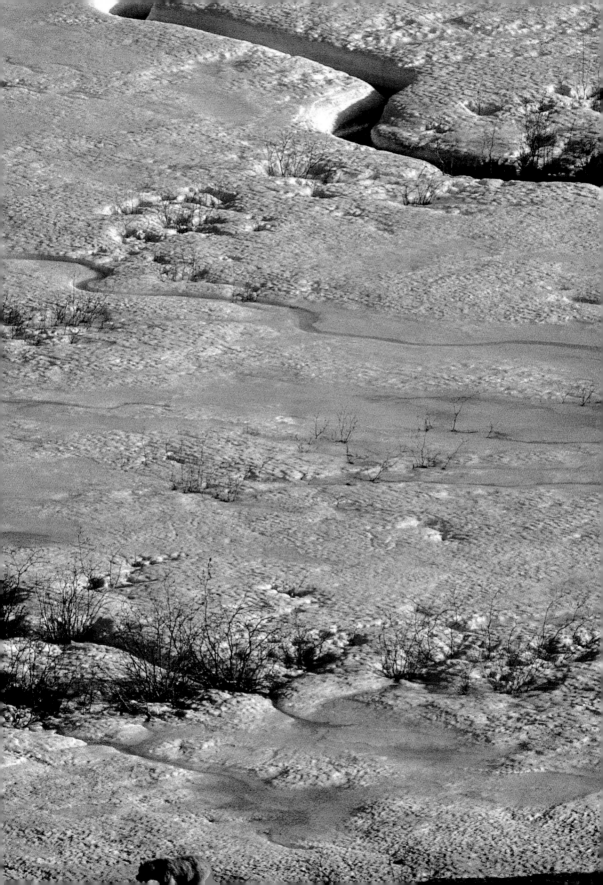

*F*or caribou, safety lies in numbers—which does not bode well for this lone juvenile (below), a straggler trailing the spring migration near Wolf Creek. The huge bands that pass through the park twice a year provide the animals' best protection against predators such as wolves and grizzlies. Yet even sheer numbers cannot protect the caribou from hazards such as river crossings, thin ice, rockfalls, stampedes, and inclement weather. Despite the dangers, the cycle of caribou migration goes on as it has for thousands of years. A rough-legged hawk (opposite), a summer resident in Ivvavik along with other raptors such as golden eagles and gyrfalcons, comes in for a landing on the spire of a tree.

FOLLOWING PAGES: *A tangle of river channels, ponds, and ice forms a collage on the coastal plain of Ivvavik National Park.*

*B*oasting one of the highest continuous rock faces in the world, 5,485-foot Mount Thor (right) in Auyuittuq National Park draws rock climbers from many nations. Cotton grass blooms in wet bogs and beside ponds during the brief Arctic summer. Steep coastal cliffs on Bylot Island as well as on northeastern Baffin Island and smaller islands in Baffin Bay and Davis Strait offer nesting sites for 1.5 million thick-billed murres (above) and other seabirds that fill the air in May and June with the rustle of wings.

FOLLOWING PAGES: Snowdrift come to life, a polar bear faces the same future as its Arctic home—wild, yet, without protection, surprisingly vulnerable. Denizens of floating pack ice, polar bears may come ashore in any of Canada's coastal Arctic national parks.

Canada's National Parks and National Park Reserves

Aulavik, Northwest Territories; 4,710 sq mi/12,199 sq km; hdqrs: General Delivery, Sachs Harbor, NT X0E 0Z0; (403) 690-3904; agreement to establish: 1992

Auyuittuq, Northwest Territories; 8,290 sq mi/21,470 sq km; hdqrs: Box 353, Pangnirtung, NT X0A 0R0; (819) 473-8828; established 1976

Banff, Alberta; 2,564 sq mi/ 6,641 sq km; hdqrs: Box 900, Banff, AL T0L 0C0; (403) 762-1500; established 1885

Bruce Peninsula, Ontario; 104 sq mi/270 sq km authorized; hdqrs: Box 189, Tobermory, ON N0H 2R0; (519) 596-2233; agreement to establish: 1987

Cape Breton Highlands, Nova Scotia; 367 sq mi/950 sq km; hdqrs: Ingonish Beach, NS B0C 1L0; (902) 224-2306; established 1936

Elk Island, Alberta; 75 sq mi/ 194 sq km; hdqrs: R.R. 1, Site 4, Fort Saskatchewan, AL T8L 2N7; (403) 992-6380; established 1913

Ellesmere Island, Northwest Territories; 14,585 sq mi/ 37,775 sq km; hdqrs: Box 353, Pangnirtung, NT X0A 0R0; (819) 473-8828; established 1988

Fathom Five, Ontario; 51 sq mi/ 132 sq km; hdqrs: Box 189, Tobermory, ON N0H 2R0; (519) 596-2233; established 1987

Forillon, Quebec; 93 sq mi/ 240 sq km; hdqrs: Box 1220, Gaspé, PQ G0C 1R0; (418) 892-5553; agreement to establish: 1970

Fundy, New Brunswick; 80 sq mi/ 206 sq km; hdqrs: Box 40, Alma, NB E0A 1B0; (506) 887-6000; established 1948

Georgian Bay Islands, Ontario; 4.6 sq mi/12 sq km; hdqrs: Box 28, Honey Harbor, ON P0E 1E0; (705) 756-2415; established 1929

Glacier, British Columbia; 521 sq mi/1,349 sq km; hdqrs: Box 350, Revelstoke, BC V0E 2S0; (604) 837-5155; established 1886

Grasslands, Saskatchewan; 350 sq mi/906 sq km; hdqrs: Box 150, Val

Marie, SK S0N 2T0; (306) 298-2257; agreement to establish: 1975

Gros Morne, Newfoundland; 697 sq mi/1,805 sq km; hdqrs: Box 130 Rocky Harbour, NF A0K 4N0; (709) 458-2417; agreement to establish: 1973

Gwaii Haanas, British Columbia; 568 sq mi/1,470 sq km; hdqrs: Box 37, Queen Charlotte City, BC V0T 1S0; (604) 559-6319; agreement to establish: 1988

Ivvavik, Yukon Territory; 3,926 sq mi/ 10,168 sq km; hdqrs: Box 1840, Inuvik, NT X0E 0T0; (403) 979-3248; established 1984

Jasper, Alberta; 4,200 sq mi/10,878 sq km; hdqrs: Box 10, Jasper, AL T0E 1E0; (403) 852-6161; established 1907

Kejimkujik, Nova Scotia; 147 sq mi/ 381 sq km; hdqrs: Box 236, Maitland Bridge, NS B0T 1B0; (902) 682-2772; established 1974

Kluane, Yukon Territory; 8,500 sq mi/22,015 sq km; hdqrs: Box 5495, Haines Junction, YT Y0B 1L0; (403) 634-2251; established 1972

Kootenay, British Columbia; 543 sq mi/ 1,406 sq km; hdqrs: Box 220, Radium Hot Springs, BC V0A 1M0; (604) 347-9615; established 1920

Kouchibouguac, New Brunswick; 92 sq mi/239 sq km; hdqrs: Kouchibouguac, NB E0A 2A0; (506) 876-2443; established 1979

La Mauricie, Quebec; 210 sq mi/ 544 sq km; hdqrs: Place Cascade, 794A 5th Street, P.O. Box 758, Shawinigan, PQ G9N 6V9; (819)

536-2638; established 1970

Mingan Archipelago, Quebec; 58 sq mi/150 sq km; hdqrs: 1303 de la Digue St., Box 1180, Havre-Saint-Pierre, PQ G0G 1P0; (418) 538-3331; established 1984

After months of winter white, patches of color explode on the tundra of Ivvavik National Park, as wildflowers such as this rare, endemic many-headed anemone rush to bloom in the short Arctic summer.

Mount Revelstoke, British Columbia; 100 sq mi/260 sq km; hdqrs: Box 350, Revelstoke, BC V0E 2S0; (604) 837-5155; established 1914

Nahanni, Northwest Territories; 1,840 sq mi/4,766 sq km; hdqrs: Box 348, Fort Simpson, NT X0E 0N0; (403)

695-3151; established 1976

North Baffin, Northwest Territories; 8,538 sq mi/22,252 sq km; hdqrs: Box 353, Pangnirtung, NT X0A 0R0; (819) 473-8828; established 1992

Pacific Rim, British Columbia; 193 sq mi/500 sq km; hdqrs: Box 280, Ucluelet, BC V0R 3A0; (604) 726-7721; agreement to establish: 1970

Point Pelee, Ontario; 6 sq mi/ 15.5 sq km; hdqrs: R.R. 1, Leamington, ON N8H 3V4; (519) 322-2365; established 1918

Prince Albert, Saskatchewan; 1,496 sq mi/3,875 sq km; hdqrs: Box 100, Waskesiu Lake, SK S0J 2Y0; (306) 663-5322; established 1927

Prince Edward Island; 12 sq mi/ 32 sq km; hdqrs: 2 Palmers Lane, Charlottetown, PE C1A 5V6; (902) 566-7050; established 1937

Pukaskwa, Ontario; 725 sq mi/ 1,878 sq km; hdqrs: Highway 627, Hattie Cove, Box 39, Heron Bay, ON P0T 1R0; (807) 229-0801; agreement to establish: 1978

Riding Mountain, Manitoba; 1,148 sq mi/2,973 sq km; hdqrs: General Delivery, Wasagaming, MB R0J 2H0; (204) 848-2811; established 1929

St. Lawrence Islands, Ontario; 3.5 sq mi/9 sq km; hdqrs: 2 County Road 5, R.R. 3, Mallorytown Landing, ON K0E 1R0; (613) 923-5261; established 1904

Terra Nova, Newfoundland; 154 sq mi/400 sq km; hdqrs: Glovertown, NF A0G 2L0; (709) 533-2801; established 1957

Vuntut, Yukon Territory; 1,699 sq mi/4,400 sq km; hdqrs: c/o Canadian Heritage, 105-300 Main St., Whitehorse, YT Y1A 2B5; (403) 667-3970; established 1995

Waterton Lakes, Alberta; 203 sq mi/ 525 sq km; office of superintendent: Waterton Park, AL T0K 2M0; (403) 859-2224; established 1895

Wood Buffalo, Alberta and Northwest Territories; 17,300 sq mi/ 44,802 sq km; hdqrs: Box 750, Fort Smith, NT X0E 0P0; (403) 872-2349; established 1922

Yoho, British Columbia; 506 sq mi/ 1,313 sq km; hdqrs.: Box 99, Field, BC V0A 1G0; (604) 343-6324; established 1886

Notes on Contributors

David Dunbar, born and reared in Saskatoon, Saskatchewan, is a graduate of Dartmouth College. Now based in Manhattan, he has contributed to a number of books about his native land, including the award-winning *Atlas of Canada.*

Born in South Carolina, contract photographer **Raymond Gehman** grew up in Virginia. He currently resides in Pennsylvania's Cumberland Valley. Assignments have taken him to Canada's Banff National Park for NATIONAL GEOGRAPHIC and Jasper for NATIONAL GEOGRAPHIC TRAVELER. He photographed Yellowstone National Park in the United States for a Special Publication.

On the Society's staff since 1971, senior writer **Tom Melham** wrote in previous Special Publications about Saskatchewan, Newfoundland, and Labrador. He also authored *John Muir's Wild America* and *Alaska's Wildlife Treasures,* in addition to single chapters for many other titles.

A specialist in wilderness areas, **Lawrence Millman** has written extensively about the North and its inhabitants. His books include *Last Places, A Kayak Full of Ghosts,* and *Our Like Will Not Be There Again.* This assignment gave him a chance to look at Canada's Pacific coast for the first time.

As a freelance photographer, **Richard Olsenius** provided coverage of Alaska, Labrador, and the Canadian Arctic for NATIONAL GEOGRAPHIC, where he is now an illustrations editor. He photographed U.S. parks for Special Publications.

Former staff member **Cynthia Russ Ramsay** explored British Columbia for the Special Publication *Canada's Incredible Coasts.* On assignment for *Great Journeys of the World,* she rode India's Palace-on-Wheels train for the "trip of a lifetime."

Jeff Rennicke, a former wilderness guide on Arctic rivers, is a freelance writer. His work appears frequently in TRAVELER and in BACKPACKER magazine, where he has been a field editor since 1989.

Senior writer **Jennifer C. Urquhart,** a staff member since 1971, has contributed to many Special Publications, including *Canada's Incredible Coasts* and *America's Great Hideaways,* which took her to national parks along Canada's coasts and in the Rocky Mountains.

Acknowledgments

The Book Division wishes to thank the individuals, groups, and organizations named or quoted in the text for their help in the preparation of this volume. We are especially grateful for the cooperation and patience of the staff of Parks Canada, Department of Canadian Heritage; in particular, Shelley Cameron, Jim Johnston, and Wayne Scott at headquarters, and the following individuals at various parks: Pierre Bertrand, Hugh Bremner, Doug Burles, Frank Burrows, Michael Burzynski, Carolyn Duchoslav, Gary Fellbaum, Bill Fisher, Kim Forster, Bill Fox, Shelley Gellatly, Todd Golumbia, G. Roger Hamilton, Ron Hamilton, Ron Hooper, Sheila Luey, Anne Marceau, Chris McCarthy, Bill McIntyre, Florence Miller, David Milne, Gary Pittman, Martin Raillard, Vicki Sahanatien, Maggie Stronge, Albert Van Dijk, Elaine Wallace, Josie Weninger, Mark Wiercinski, Barbara J. Wilson, and Brian R. Wood.

In addition, we are grateful to Steve Blasco, Jeffrey M. Breiwick, the Canadian Embassy Information Center, Catherine Cockney, Ron L. DiLabio, Alan Edie, Edward Elanik, John Enrico, Penny Ericson, Lorna N. Gould, Derek Green, Peggy Jay, Helen Kerfoot, Mildred Klassen, James W. Kurth, Moira J. F. Lemon, Johnny Mikes, Jim Muir, Paul Paquet, Brian Patton, Randall R. Reeves, T. E. Reimchen, Miles Richardson, Sr., Allen Smith, Cameron Spence, Julie Storr, Douglas R. Urquhart, and George E. Watson.

Additional Reading

Readers may wish to consult the *National Geographic Index* for related articles, as well as the following titles: Marianne Boelscher, *The Curtain Within: Haida Social and Mythical Discourse;* Derek E. G. Briggs, Douglas H. Erwin, Frederick J. Collier, *The Fossils of the Burgess Shale;* L. N. Carbyn et al., *Wolves, Bison…;* David Dunbar, *The Outdoor Traveler's Guide: Canada;* Ben Gadd, *Handbook of the Canadian Rockies;* Kevin McNamee, *The National Parks of Canada;* National Geographic Society, *National Parks of North America: Canada, United States, Mexico;* Brian Patton and Bart Robinson, *The Canadian Rockies Trail Guide.*

Index

Boldface indicates illustrations.

Library of Congress ⊂IP Data

Exploring Canada's Spectacular National Parks / photographed by Raymond Gehman ; prepared by the Book Division ; [contributing authors, David Dunbar ... et al. ; contributing photographer, Richard Olsenius].
    p. cm.
    Includes bibliographical references (p.) and index.
    ISBN 0-7922-2735-2. — ISBN 0-7922-2963-0 (deluxe)
    1. National parks and reserves—(Canada) 2. National parks and reserves—Canada—Pictorial works. I. Gehman, Raymond. II. Dunbar, David. III. National Geographic Society (U.S.) Book Division.
F1011.E97 1995
917.1—dc20
                                        95-24289
                                        ⊂IP

Composition for this book by the National Geographic Society Book Division, with the assistance of the Typographic section of National Geographic Production Services, Pre-Press Division. Printed and bound by R. R. Donnelley & Sons, Willard, Ohio. Color separations by Digital Color Image, Pennsauken, N.J.; Graphic Art Service, Inc., Nashville, Tenn.; and Penn Colour Graphics, Inc., Huntingdon Valley, Pa. Dust jacket printed by Miken Systems, Inc., Cheektowaga, N.Y.